"Beautifully and s........., w........ . . . . *Senator Herron's stories quicken our own memories, kindle our hopes, and strengthen our resolve to joyfully and courageously live our own stories.*"

—Bishop Kenneth L. Carder,
The United Methodist Church,
Nashville Area, Tennessee,
and Memphis Conferences

"*Roy Herron's marvelous stories will not only touch the hearts and souls of his sons. They will motivate and inspire all of us who have been blessed to have shared a life of loving families, caring friends, and everyday heroes. This book will truly be 'held dear' by everyone who reads it.*"

—Bill Haltom, *ABA Journal*

"*A wise, humane, and beautifully written picture of a family and a segment of its life and joys and trials. Full of humor, candid in identifying the faults and foibles of Southern life, it manages to affirm cardinal American virtues without a trace of moralism. The book will bring pleasure and insight to many children and their parents.*"

—Walter Harrelson, Professor Emeritus,
Vanderbilt University Divinity School

THINGS HELD DEAR

THINGS HELD DEAR

Soul Stories for My Sons

ROY BRASFIELD HERRON

Westminster John Knox Press
Louisville, Kentucky

Scripture quotations from the Revised Standard Version of the Bible are copyright © 1946, 1952, 1971, and 1973 by the Division of Christian Education of the National Council of the Churches of Christ in the U.S.A. and are used by permission.

Book design by Jeff Wincapaw
Cover design by Night and Day Design
Cover illustration courtesy of author

First edition
Published by Westminster John Knox Press
Louisville, Kentucky

This book is printed on acid-free paper that meets the American National Standards Institute Z39.48 standard.

PRINTED IN THE UNITED STATES OF AMERICA
99 00 01 02 03 04 05 06 07 08 — 10 9 8 7 6 5 4 3 2 1

Cataloguing in Publication information is on file at the Library of Congress

*For Dad who taught courage,
for Mother who teaches love,
and especially for John, Rick and BJ
who daily teach joy*

Acknowledgments

I owe so many that I hesitate to thank some, knowing I cannot tell of others I would and should. I ask forgiveness from those not thanked here.

First, I thank the people who hired me to represent them in the Tennessee Senate. Every day you share values and experiences and I am richer for all you share. As Governor McWherter taught and you prove, representing you is a great privilege.

Larry and Betsy McGehee revealed the power and possibilities of words and their writing first made me want to write. Bill Haltom also was and is an example as an extraordinary writer, as well as the father of my godson, Will.

John Egerton and Will Campbell both took time from their writing to read mine, treated me like family, and set the standards both for writing and living. Will also helped create our family, by officiating at our wedding and baptizing our twins, as did Susan Ford Wiltshire who also showed how writing can fit with family and profession and more.

When it came time to start this book, Mike Kopp provided inspiration, guidance and sound counsel. Peter Coughlan kindly pulled together articles and essays and helped create the first draft. If not for Mike and Peter, I'd never have begun.

Josephine Binkley, my legislative assistant, worked extra hard (even for her) so I could put in less office overtime. Joanne Pierce, my long-time legal assistant, took care of clients and me and helped with the manuscript. Mary Gardner and Beverly Pierpoint of our law office also helped in numerous ways. My partner, Bill Neese, carried an extra legal load while I rewrote and rewrote.

Sarah Fortenberry was the first editor to recognize there might be a book in my manuscript. She and her talented writer husband Robert Benson provided encouragement, editing and the title.

Other special friends helped in numerous ways. I especially thank Pattie, Joe and Gwin Anderson, Don Beisswenger, Bob Cooper, Russell Caldwell, Bonnie Cochran, Mike Cox, Jan and Dennis Dugan, Emmett Edwards, Amy and Ricky Finney, Jim and Lucia Gilliland, Walter Haden, Johnny and Mary Howard Hayes, Joe and Susan Hill, Jan Keeling, Joni Laney, Laurie and Tom Lee, Representative Mark Maddox, Lane and Jon McLelland, Mark and Janis McNeely, Governor Ned McWherter, GranFran and L.J. Miller, Susan Neese, Kim and Johnny Simpson, Byron Trauger, Greg Waldrop, and David Waters.

Stephanie Egnotovich, Executive Editor with

ACKNOWLEDGMENTS *ix*

Westminster John Knox Press, made this book happen. She is the best editor and friend a writer could hope for and I am deeply grateful to her. Her colleagues at Westminster also have been most kind and I especially thank Michael Cirone, Jennifer Cox, Bill Falvey, Laura Lutz, Annie McClure, and Tom Maiuro.

My beloved siblings, Ben and Dean Herron and Betsye Herron Hickman, all assisted with certain stories. I am blessed to be theirs. My mother shared openly and listened patiently as I read back what she'd said. She is unspeakably wonderful.

I've known almost from the moment I met her in a hotel lobby in Atlanta, a meeting she tries to explain away as a church conference, that Nancy Carol Miller was extraordinary. For a dozen years she's been my bride and the greatest blessing of my life. Dad used to say, "It's a sorry fellow who can't out-marry himself." Clearly, I out-married myself considerably. Without my law and life partner, this book would not be.

I think it was Yogi Berra or Casey Stengel (one of those Yankees from New York who think *we* talk funny) who said at an event honoring him, "I'd like to thank the people who made this necessary." Similarly, I'd like to thank the boys who made this book necessary. John, Rick and BJ have a wonderful way with words and have been kind and patient as I have tried to find my way with these words. They are, quite frankly, the best boys I ever knew. Thank goodness they take after their mother. And thank goodness I am blessed to be their father.

Contents

Foreword

Governor Ned McWherter[1]

This is a book of stories about values. It is a book for times when you want to think about values like courage or freedom. Or the values in experiences like farming, or hunting, or being family. It is a book to turn to when things are good, or bad, or you just want to think about how things are—and how they should be.

Friends can talk about this book in places ranging from a Sunday School class to a duck blind, from a country store to a city restaurant. It can be read and discussed a chapter at a time.

I have known Roy Herron all his life. He grew up down the street from me and when I ran for Governor he took my seat in the Tennessee House of Representatives. I have known for a long time that Roy is a good and

[1]Ned R. McWherter served as the Governor of Tennessee from 1987 to 1995. Before that he served as Speaker of the Tennessee House of Representatives for fourteen years, longer than any other person.

1

honest man and an able and effective legislator. What I
have not known is that he is a fine writer. Roy writes of
uncommon people we commonly know. He tells stories
of courageous soldiers and disabled veterans, manly
hunters and little boys, daredevil girls and brave women
survivors, sports stars and benchwarmers, proud
Confederate descendants and pained sons of slaves, the
dying and those who live forever.

His stories include experiences familiar to many of us,
including Scouting and farming. Here also are true tales
of faith and love found in institutions such as political
parties and churches, each with its loud evangelists and
quiet believers.

As you read, you will find the values of the same
good folks who have been so kind to you and me:

- Families. Those who start loving you before you are
  born, and whom you love even after they die and
  until you die. Those who make your life most worth
  living.
- Neighbors. Including those who may not be blood kin
  but treat you as their own. When you are young, they
  know more about you than you do, and they care
  about you always.
- Religious people. The people and pastors that trust in
  the Lord. I suspect they taught Roy more by their
  lives than all he read about in divinity schools.
- Patriotic people. Folks who do not just talk about
  patriotism, but practice it. People like Roy's father,
  who went off to war and came back wounded and
  who himself was an honorable public servant and a
  fine judge.

Roy has taken the best of our values. In this book he gives our values back to us, though often with insights that make the familiar seem new. What he has written is worth reading. Here are people and values that make a difference.

Preface

The photo on the dust jacket of this book is of my father and either my brother Ben or me. The baby's hair looks light, which points toward Ben, but the baby's so fat it probably was me.

My father was holding his son. The son was trying to hold to his father. Each held what was dear to him.

In the background is the house my grandparents built when Mother was a child. It is where she bore two of her children and where she has lived seven of her eight decades. It is the house where I grew up.

In the foreground is the spot where Dad, when he first returned home from World War II, dropped his crutches, fell to the ground, and kissed the earth.

It is a black and white photo from the fifties. For many of us who grew up in the fifties and sixties, they were black and white times.

To be sure, shades of gray came, and Technicolor and psychedelic colors—and now even computerized colors. But when I was growing up in the South, many things and values were black and white, not gray, and certainly not Technicolor.

Those values came from families who loved us, neighbors that cared for us, institutions that nurtured us, experiences that blessed us. And that is what this book is about.

This book is about growing up in the South. Here are stories of the people and experiences that were and are mine. But you will find your people and your experiences here or not far away—not as far away as you might first think.

These are the stories so special to me that I call them "soul stories." They are of the souls that shaped my own and they are the stories that stir my soul yet.

They are soul stories for my sons, because sons are what God gave Nancy and me and because Nancy says I don't know how to make little girls. I think the stories can teach not only boys and men, but also those who marry them, bear them, care about them.

As we begin this new millennium, I want our children—and yours—to know stories from the past to help shape their future. I want my sons to know that in the midst of the grays and the colors, some things are black and white. Things like loving your family, caring for your neighbors, believing in God, working hard, doing your best. These are things held dear.

ONE

Legs of Fire

*F*or as long as I can remember, Mother has pointed out where they were on the road when they heard the news. It was late 1941, a dozen years before I was born. They were in a black Ford coupe, their first car with a radio and glass side windows. They were going home to Dresden after Sunday dinner at Dad's parents' home in Greenfield.

My brother Dean, four years old, was standing on the back seat and leaning over into the front seat. Mother and Dad were touching and loving my brother as Dad drove, since Dean was not yet sure he liked his two-month-old sister, Betsye, then cradled in Mother's arms. The baby was dressed up with a little bonnet that matched both her dress and the shoes she had kicked off. It was the baby girl's first trip out of Dresden and

Mother still recalls, more than half a century later, the minute details etched into her memory by the news.

Dad was twenty-nine and Mom was twenty-five, but like millions of Americans they matured considerably when they heard the news flash on the radio: Japanese planes had bombed American ships and sailors at some place called Pearl Harbor. The first report said some lives were lost. By the time they neared Dresden, a journey of just twelve miles, another report brought details of the devastation.

* * *

A lot of younger men went to war first. Dad continued to farm and serve as clerk and master for the Chancery Court and he joined the Tennessee State Guard. By the time Uncle Sam wrote my father late in 1943, he was in his thirties. "Greetings" the telegram began. He was summoned in what one of his fellow draftees recalls as the first and perhaps the only draft of fathers.

Just because he had received the draft notice did not mean he had to go. He still was farming and working as a government official, and I'm told both situations permitted deferments. But even without deferments, there was politics, and he was well-connected.

My father was of two minds. He had wanted to enlist, but his father-in-law had pressured him not to, not to leave his wife and children. But Dad had long felt it was his duty to defend our country and freedom, and he yearned to do what he ought to do. On the other hand, who in his right mind wanted to leave a beautiful wife and two precious little children, perhaps never to come home to them? No, of course my father did not want to

go. He wanted to stay with his family more than anything, except for one thing.

He knew if he did not go, someone else, one of his
neighbors, would have to take his place, for each county had quotas to meet. If not he, another Weakley
Countian would have to go. If not he, someone he probably knew would have to go—and might not come back.
How could he ever look in the eyes of their wives and
sons and daughters? And since he would never know
for sure which soldier had taken his place, how would
he face all of the widows and fatherless children?

* * *

In January of 1944 he went to Fort McClellan,
Alabama, for basic training. His advanced training
would come in Europe under fire.

Another draftee with Dad, Needham Schraeder, was
from nearby McKenzie. Dad and Schraeder quickly
became friends, and so did their wives. Schraeder's
wife, my mother, and my older brother and sister trav-
eled together to Fort McClellan to visit the men.

At Fort McClellan, the troops paraded for the visitors.
Children and wives looked for their fathers and husbands among the dozens of rows of identically dressed
soldiers. My brother, then seven years old, finally spied
Dad and yelled, "My Daddy! My Daddy!" Though
under orders not to look at or respond to the crowd in
any way, the soldiers still stole glimpses. Dad winked,
all the invitation Dean needed to run onto the parade
grounds.

A local druggist had arranged for my family and the
Schraeders to stay with two sisters in their big old

house. When Dad and Schraeder got off for the weekend, both families rushed over there. Mother and Mrs.
Schraeder spread a sheet on the floor of one bedroom
and covered it with good country cooking they'd
brought from home—biscuits, sorghum molasses, country ham, turnip greens, black-eyed peas, green beans,
three types of pickles, cakes, pies, and pears from the
farm. Army food may have been nutritious—and for
many Depression-poor boys the best food they had ever
had—but for Schraeder and Dad, farm boys from
Tennessee, nothing compared to the treats from home.
And when the feast was done, the sisters kindly offered
to show the children the town and discreetly took them
away for a while.

* * *

After they finished training at Fort McClellan in June
1944, Dad and Schraeder came home for a week, then
left again. The two couples drove to a nearby town and
picked up another soldier, a boy who would be killed in
the war.

Then they drove east to Nashville. There at Union
Station, hundreds of soldiers waited for troop trains.
They waited for hours, patiently, because no one was in
a hurry to depart. Finally, though, it was time for Dad to
leave. He promised mother he would be home soon, but
he and Mother both knew that would not be so—not
unless he was gravely wounded or dead.

Soon Dad, Schraeder, and thousands more were on
ships headed for England. Dad joined the Ninth
Infantry, the last of the regular army divisions activated,
whose ranks had been filled by the Selective Service but
thinned in earlier combat.

*   *   *

Dad got to England in July of 1944. He had barely landed in England before he was on a landing craft headed for Normandy. As they crossed the English Channel, over the loudspeaker came the voice of Roy Acuff singing, "The Great Speckled Bird." Years later, Dad would remember that no son of the South, and few from anywhere else, had dry eyes as Roy Acuff sang that Grand Ole Opry favorite and their thoughts returned to home. How many times had Acuff sung to him and his bride on Saturday nights? Would he ever hear the Opry again?

*   *   *

They hit Omaha Beach and before long were fighting in the hedgerows. Most days Dad and his buddies left their gear and fieldpacks in trucks that followed their advances. For some reason, one day his buddies and he wore their fieldpacks. And that day their own artillery fire, "friendly fire," came right in on them.

An artillery shell landed so close that it instantly killed one man next to Dad and severely wounded another, who soon died. Dad's fieldpack was torn to pieces. His shovel, bedroll, and Bible saved him, a piece of shrapnel shredding the Bible. Dad always knew that without the backpack and its contents the shrapnel would have hit his lungs rather than his shoulder. At the field hospital a doctor told him he was lucky, saying "You've got a ticket home." But Dad wasn't going anywhere; he wasn't leaving his buddies. He talked the medical personnel into patching him up and letting him go, and he hurried forward to rejoin his unit.

A few days later he was wounded again, but again it could have been much worse. For thousands, it was. So on he fought with his buddies, all part of the Ninth Infantry that famed war correspondent Ernie Pyle once called "a beautiful machine. "

Did the soldiers always know what they fought for? Maybe some did, maybe to others the words "freedom" and "home" were enough. Historian Stephen Ambrose in his *Citizen Soldiers* reports a soldier who, upon discovering the horrors behind the gates of a concentration camp, said, "Now I know why I am here."

But those discoveries were still months ahead. In the meantime, Dad and his fellow soldiers must have wondered why in God's name they were killing and trying to avoid being killed, why in heaven's name they were enduring hell on earth. The Germans used an awesome array of weapons and soldiers against them, often defending the impenetrable hedgerows by setting up tanks and machine guns right in their midst. German artillery frequently was pre-set to deliver precisely on our soldiers just as they entered fields. The shells killed many instantly and made many wounded wish for death to come quickly.

What those men endured and overcame many would never talk about. And it was only by grace that some survived.

* * *

The Ninth Infantry beat off a series of counter-attacks and then joined in the chase. In late August they pushed east, across the Seine River at Melun, then northeast to the Marne River without opposition. The next day they swept through historic Chateau-Thierry.

About three months after Dad finished basic training, on September 2, the Ninth claimed to be the first Allied force to start the liberation of Belgium. In every town the GIs were greeted by throngs of happy people who had waited four long years for freedom. The Ninth pushed on toward a place called Dinant and the Meuse River.

Soon they would go forward without my father.

* * *

By September, almost none of the original men of Dad's company, the men he started across France with, were still with him. My brother recalls Dad saying that he was one of about three still fighting in that company of 150 men. His unit came to the Meuse River and Dinant. Three decades later this would be the first place my brother Ben and I visited on our trip to Europe. We saw such a beautiful town and such a peaceful river then that it was hard to imagine what Dad had seen.

But back then the Nazis were across the river on the mountain, firing down on the Americans. The mortar shell landed beside Dad, so close that it is probably what saved his life. The shrapnel expanded out in an upward "V" trajectory. Because the mortar shell hit so close, most of the shrapnel got him in the legs instead of higher in his body where the wounds would have been fatal.

A brave medic, just a kid, scrambled over and threw his body over Dad to protect him from additional fire, and then he pulled Dad under some farm equipment. When Dad awoke, he was in a field hospital tent. The rain was pouring down and he saw water running underneath his cot. The medical personnel working on him were standing in water up to their ankles.

* * *

They shipped him back to England and took him to a hospital near Manchester. Fighting the Nazis was over for him. Fighting to survive, however, had just begun.

My father's legs were so seriously injured that the doctors wanted to amputate them, but he refused to let them. So they operated time and again, picking out the dirt, debris and shrapnel that did not erupt and ooze out of his flesh on its own. Most of the large pieces of shrapnel were below his waist, but some smaller pieces were in his back, neck and head. One piece remained in his earlobe. When I was a boy he would let me feel it.

Three weeks after he was wounded, he wrote home.

Sept. 27, 1944
Dear Mary, Dean & Betsye,

 Gene Crawford has just been in to see me & boy, was I glad to see him. We really enjoyed talking about Dresden. He is going to send Howard Cashon to see me tomorrow. He also told me that Harold Cashon, Charles (Bear Creek) Speight & one of Kelly Finch's boys are in this neighborhood and so I hope to get to see all of them in the near future. If we all can get together England had better give its soul to the Lord for we will take the rest of it. You can't imagine how one enjoys seeing someone from home.

 Gene told me that Harold Cashon was wounded in the foot, Howard in the shoulder & that Charles Speight had had malaria but I don't know where the Finch boy was hit. Gene also told me that one of the Finch boys was missing in action & that he understood that Mark Melton was a German prisoner. I gave him some of that good old

Alexander & Brasfield candy. He told me was expecting to be a papa in about three months.

I am improving every day, and I hope you are all well. Mary, dear, I love you with all my heart. You are the sweetest girl in the world. I am indeed lucky to have such a sweet and lovely wife. Belong all to me and love our children for me.

Dean, I love you so very, very good. You are the sweetest, smartest boy in the world and I love you with all my heart. Take good care of mother & Betsye for me.

Betsye, belong all to your daddy. He loves you with all his heart.

> **With all my love, I am**
> **Your husband & dad**
> **Pvt. Clarence G. Herron**

P.S. I love you all with all my heart.

* * *

A month later Dad wrote home again:

Oct. 28, 1944
Darling Mary,

Today is our 10th wedding anniversary, and my thoughts are all of you.

Darling, you are the sweetest wife any man ever had and I love you more and more each passing day. I am mighty fortunate to have won such a sweet, adorable girl for a wife.

In my dreams, I will see your beautiful brown eyes, I will feel your sweet red lips pressed to mine and I will stroke your soft hair. Even though we are a good many miles apart, tonight I feel your sweet spirit very close to me.

*I will never find the words to tell you just how much I
love you, but when we are reunited I will do my best to
prove by actions just how dearly I love you.*

Belong all to me every bit. With all my love

**Your husband,
Grooms Herron**

With the letter, my father also sent a photo of a group
of hospital patients. A nurse stood behind him as he sat
in a wheelchair, a blanket over his legs. Mother showed
the photo to friends and soon our town buzzed with the
talk that Dad had lost his legs. Otherwise, people said,
why would there be a blanket over his legs—or where
his legs should have been?

Mother, knowing Dad's inclination to shield her from
bad news and his pride that wanted no pity, thought he
was trying to keep the amputations a secret. She wrote
him about what people were saying and asked for the
bad news. Although he wrote back denying his legs
were gone, she still doubted his reassurances.

During his months in the English hospital, as infections ravaged his legs and almost killed him, he wasted
down to 89 pounds. A pretty good-sized farm boy,
almost six feet tall, he weighed less than his tiny five-
foot mother-in-law.

* * *

Finally, after five months in an English hospital, an
ocean liner, a troop ship early in the war then serving as
a hospital ship, brought him back to New York City.
Although he objected strenuously, he was carried off the
ship on a stretcher. From New York, a train took him to
Blackstone, Virginia, to yet another hospital.

Mother soon went to Blackstone. When she got off the train, she looked for her husband. She saw a man standing, balancing with crutches, casts on his legs up to his hips. She did not recognize the man, so thin was he. Then she looked into those blue eyes and saw her husband.

* * *

He remained in a Virginia military hospital for five more months and additional operations. More surgeries, however, could not repair the damage to the nerves in his legs. These doctors also recommended double amputations. He still refused, even though his legs were so worthless that much of the time he was confined to a bed or a wheelchair, suffering enormous pain.

Finally, ten months after he was wounded, trains brought him home to Tennessee. When he got out of the car in Dresden, my brother Dean watched Dad slowly climb the three concrete steps in front of the house. At the top of the steps, Dad dropped his crutches and let himself fall forward. He caught himself on his hands. Then he kissed the ground.

* * *

Though Tennessee was the Promised Land, the land he had sought for so many months, and though the joy of being home was great, so still was the pain. It was constant, unrelenting. He told Mother his legs felt like they were on fire every waking moment. And there were not enough other moments. At times Dad would say, "I'd just be better off dead. I can't take this any more."

Infections still frequently raged in his legs and Dr.

Paul Wilson treated him with the penicillin that repeatedly saved his life. But the doctor also treated him for
more than his physical injuries, for Dad talked with Dr.
Wilson about suicide. The physician tried to shame him
into going on.

"Grooms, don't you have something to be thankful
for every day?"

"Yes," Dad replied quietly.

"You have Mary and the children. Think of what it
would mean to them if you did what you're thinking
about."

Dad said nothing. Then the doctor added a more
hopeful note, "Maybe someday we can get rid of this
pain."

Paul Wilson reported this conversation to two people,
my mother and her father, Mr. Roy, who was Dr.
Wilson's good friend as well as a pharmacist. Mom, Dad,
my brother, and sister were still living with Mom's parents, and Mother noticed that her father chose this time
to remove his guns. He said he was taking them to the
drug store to get them away from the children, but
Mother knew he was taking them away from Dad,
whose despair at his pain threatened him daily.

* * *

Dad endured. Somehow. When he came home from
the hospitals, he returned to his job as clerk and master
to the Chancery Court in Weakley County. As he
watched lawyers try cases in that court, he knew he
could do that as well as some and better than many.

The G.I. Bill put him through law school. That and the
tolerance of many kind people. The chancellor and citi-

zens in Weakley County let him continue as clerk and master while he went to law school four days a week almost 200 miles away. Dad paid an able deputy clerk to do most of the work, all of it on the days he was gone. The deans and teachers at the law school let him skip Friday classes. His family was willing to put up with his being gone half the time and studying hard when he was with them.

I was born about the same time he got the news that he had passed the bar exam. He hung out his shingle, a 41-year-old disabled veteran and father of three, and started over again.

From the beginning of his military service to the beginning of his new life, a decade had passed.

T W O

Guns and Guys

*W*hen I was born, my parents brought me home to a house with a history of shotguns in it and bird dogs behind it. I never knew the grandparents who had built our home. But I learned early on that Mr. Roy had loved to hunt quail and shoot trap. Mom still talked about the time her father had won a big trap shooting contest against shooters from all over the South.

My father's father, Mr. Clarence, did not hunt much, but in his 1954 Chevrolet pickup truck (which came out the same autumn I did) he often carried a .410 double barrel shotgun. He used it mostly to kill snakes and impress young boys. He died while I was young, but I still hear him warning me never to point a gun at anyone. Not even if I thought the gun was unloaded. "Always be careful with guns, son. It's the unloaded guns that kill people."

My older brother, Dean, shot rifles in competition. He won more medals, trophies, guns, and other prizes than any shooter I have ever known. He was named an All-American with the best shooters in the National Guard from all over the country. He competed against America's top shooters, both civilian and military, at Camp Perry, Ohio, sort of the Super Bowl of shooting. He won there, too.

Then there was Dad. He had been a hunter and a fine shooter as well. But after 1944, he'd been hospitalized and confined to a wheelchair. Then he struggled to get around on crutches. Then walked with a cane. Finally, he got some special shoes and put the cane in the closet. Then Dad decided that in order to raise right his second crop of children, born sixteen and nineteen years after his first, he was going to have to hunt again and teach us how, too.

When I was nine, Dad and my older brother Dean took me to a skeet range. They helped me figure out how to hold Dean's 16-gauge Browning Automatic. Then they gave me the easiest, going-away shots. After I broke five clay pigeons out of the first six, they announced that maybe it was getting close to the time when I could go hunting.

A few months later, on September 1st, Dad took me hunting. It was still dark that school morning when Dad got me up to go squirrel hunting. I kept hunting and hunting but did not get a squirrel, something that is still hard for me to do even now, given my weak eyes and noisy feet in the woods. But he had borrowed a Remington pump 20-gauge for me that he explained had belonged to the grandfather for whom I was named. Just to hold that shotgun was enough that morning.

When I got to school, a little late, I sure had something to tell my fifth-grade classmates. Then Dad came back at lunchtime and took me off again. Missing so much school that day, already I could see why folks liked to hunt.

As dove season opened that afternoon, Dad sat on a small stool and I knelt beside him as we watched for doves. We were at the edge of a cornfield, trees behind us and a war in front of us. It seemed like a thousand guns were firing. Lead shot frequently peppered the ground around us. Occasionally I'd feel it hit my clothing and even bare skin. I wondered if I would survive, at least without being wounded. Dad just said to look down when the incoming shot arrived. He didn't have to tell me twice.

It did not take Dad long to get his limit of twelve doves. In fact, it just took thirteen doves flying close enough for him to shoot. Meanwhile, I could not believe those rascals could fly so fast—and always know when I was about to shoot so they would swoop and swerve. My barrel moved in endless figure eights. "Lead them," Dad coached me. "Lead them as far as you think you should, and then that much further again. Then if you miss them, you'll know you still probably shot behind them and need to lead them more."

He explained some of the physics and told me to swing with and through the doves. My own theory was that if I threw up enough lead, surely something eventually would fall.

After going through a box of twenty-five shells, I had knocked down but three of the darters. My three for twenty-five did not exactly compare favorably with Dad's twelve for thirteen shooting. But he was bragging on me and telling me how I was getting the hang of it. I even began to believe him. The next box of shells went better, though I didn't get the limit that day.

But by the time the war stopped and we headed home, Dad had a hunting companion. Then came duck season.

* * *

The night before we first went duck hunting, I could not fall asleep. Moments after I finally did, Dad was shaking me. "Get up, son. Time for duck hunters to go."

I hadn't gotten up at 3:30 A.M. since I was tiny and used to fall asleep in front of the television about six at night. But there I was, hustling to get ready by four o'clock, so they wouldn't leave me. When I went in the kitchen, Mother was handing Dad a couple of grocery sacks full of food, asking Dad if he was sure we had enough to eat. She asked me if I was sure I had enough clothes on. I was bundled so much I looked like the Pillsbury dough boy topped with a new Herter's mail order hunting coat. "Yes, ma'am," I patiently replied.

Then Dad's friend Elton Drysdale knocked on the back door. And we were gone. We drove the hour to Reelfoot Lake in Elton's big Ford pickup, me snuggled in between Elton and Dad, leaning on Dad, his arm over my shoulder.

At Samburg, a town of 450 citizens right on Reelfoot Lake, the little restaurant was filled with men in hunting clothes. They were loud and boisterous. The waitresses were quick. They brought country ham, biscuits, and scrambled eggs, and I was happier than ever. So far I liked duck hunting even better than squirrel and dove hunting.

The night before, we had discovered I'd outgrown my boots. Dad had asked if I wanted to wear shoes with a couple of pairs of socks, but I knew hunters wore boots. In the restaurant, as Dad watched me cram my feet into the boots, he again suggested shoes with extra socks. But no, that wasn't for me.

We walked down to a boat shed filled with dozens of little wooden canoe-like boats. We loaded our guns and supplies in two Reelfoot lake "stumpjumpers." The boats, Dad explained, would slide or bounce over cypress stumps and logs in the swampy, shallow lake and keep on going. I got into the second boat—the one without a motor that the guide tied by a thin rope to the first one. The morning was so cold that by the time we started out in the darkness into the north wind and spray, my feet already were freezing.

The lead boat had a Briggs & Stratton engine, like a lawnmower motor, only five horsepower, if that. That little engine pulled us slowly through the whitecapping, rough water. As we crept around cypress trees and over stumps, my feet got colder. And colder.

Finally, I told Dad my feet were freezing. He did not have to remind me he had tried to get me to wear shoes. But he did. Then he suggested I wiggle my toes. I wiggled as much as I could, but the boots were too tight for me to wiggle much. I kicked my heels on the floor of the boat until it hurt too much to do that any more.

I felt more cold than I had ever felt, and tears came to my eyes. I wished I were home. We went past blind after blind. When would we ever get to ours?

When we finally did, Elton helped me crawl out of the boat. Dad seemed unconcerned. He loaded his gun and began looking for ducks in the disappearing darkness. Sonny Cochran, our guide, got the small charcoal stove going, and Elton seated me next to the stove. He slipped my boots off and gently rubbed my feet with his big carpenter's hands.

Looking back, I guess Dad was embarrassed. Embarrassed that he had brought a boy too young to take it. Maybe embarrassed that he had failed to get me equipped right. But if he was feeling bad then, he sure was not showing it. So I felt even worse.

Elton kept rubbing my feet and holding them near the charcoal stove, talking just as gently as he rubbed. Tears rolled down my cheeks. Eventually, as Elton explained to Dad that he had never seen colder feet and that he thought my feet had even been a little frost-bitten, both my feet and my feelings started to warm. Over the next couple of hours, I warmed up even more, thanks to the little stove, a thermos of hot chocolate, lots of hot, grilled tenderloin, and, oh yes, shooting at some ducks.

When I finally was feeling pretty good, they explained the First Duck Hunt Rule. It was simple: On your first duck hunt, either you kill a duck or you get thrown in the lake. They seemed serious about their rule, too, explaining that had been the rule all their lives—in fact, since even before they started hunting.

I was not too worried at first, but then again you never knew about these guys. When I asked if it was really a rule, they all vowed that it was. The First Duck Hunt Rule.

Elton finally whispered to me that his approach was to shoot a lot and, if anything fell, "claim it." Huh? "Just claim it," he whispered, bending low over me so no one else could hear. "If you're the first to claim you shot it, then it's yours." He winked down at me.

Dad spotted the next bunch of ducks and Sonny Cochran, our guide, began to call them. Around and around they circled, talking back to Sonny as they pitched in low. "Get 'em boys!" Sonny cried. I jumped up on the two wooden Coke cases they'd put in front of me so I could see over the side of the blind. I finally saw the ducks and pulled the trigger on Granddad's pump-gun. Several ducks fell, and I yelled loud enough to be heard all the way back at the restaurant, "I got that one! I got him!"

Elton backed me up. "You sure did. You got that greenhead there," he said, pointing to a mallard drake he had shot.

Sonny and Dad immediately starting arguing that they'd gotten that one. But Elton defended me. "No, the boy got that one. I saw him."

Eventually they allowed that I might not have to be thrown in the icy lake. Not unless, of course, I violated another one of the Rules of Duck Hunting.

What were the other rules? They'd tell me if I broke one, Sonny said with a smile. I tried hard to be as good as a ten-year-old boy could be. By the end of the day, they had me believing that I actually had brought down the greenhead.

Most of the time I was eating or shooting, though when I wasn't I thought about and dreaded the trip back. But in the late afternoon sunlight with feet charcoal-toasted from the fire, socks thoroughly dried, boots loosened and toes wiggling like crazy from the moment I crawled back in the boat, it was much warmer than the trip out. By the time we got to the bank, Dad had a duck hunting companion, too.

I was ten years old. The tough times as an adolescent were just ahead.

* * *

Those adolescent times did get pretty rough, as I tried to become an adult, independent of parents. I ran with my friends, a pretty tame bunch by today's standards, but still capable of violating lots of laws and getting into much mischief. I pushed the limits, most all the limits, and especially those whose violation meant excitement. I shudder to think about the other trouble I'd have found if through those adolescent years Dad and I had not kept hunting together. Sometimes that was about the only way he could get my ear, or get me to talk, either. Sometimes that was about the only thing I would do with him.

I remember the afternoon he wanted me to go with him to the farm to work, but I had planned to play basketball with friends. He insisted I go, but I sulked so much that before we had gone a full block, he slammed on the brakes. "Get out!"

He was so angry that I immediately backed up, "No, I'll go. I'll go." His blue eyes still flashed. "No, you won't. Get out. Get out *right now*!" I got out. And for days he acted like I did not exist. He did not speak to me. He did not speak about me in my presence. He totally ignored me.

Then one day Mother told me Dad wanted me to go quail hunting with him at the farm, if I wanted to go. I did and we went. And we moved on. Moved on, with hunting the means or the excuse that let us come together again.

Through those years, I found a lot of my excitement from hunting. Sometimes too much excitement—in fact, sometimes fear and once something approaching terror.

One afternoon my friend Sammy and I got our parents to drop us off at a river bottom. It was snowing when we set out walking with our rifles, not quite sure what we were hunting but hoping maybe for a rabbit in the snow or a squirrel in the woods. It was snowing so hard that it was too pretty to stay inside anyway. We didn't know it was going to be the largest snowstorm of our lives.

We walked all afternoon, having a great time in the beautiful white that was transforming the world as we walked through it. As the day dimmed and the darkness came, we became ready to find something that looked familiar. We knew we should already have crossed the highway we had thought was ahead of us. We walked on and on and still there were no highways, houses or even barns.

When the night grew late enough, the snow deep enough, and the cold bitter enough, I'd had all the danger I wanted and then some. I feared we might die. We plunged along in the drifts, falling repeatedly, pushing on. Three or so hours after dark, Sammy said he thought he saw a light. I thought he was hallucinating. Fortunately, he wasn't.

By the time we found the farmhouse, our fathers,

Sammy's brother, and the sheriff's deputies had been looking for us for quite a while. They were about ready to call out the National Guard to join the search for the boys or the bodies.

* * *

When I was about twelve, Dad bought an old, used trailer and put it in Samburg beside Reelfoot Lake. Around duck season, my family lived there more than at home.

One Christmas, Mom and Dad got my younger brother Ben and me a Reelfoot Lake boat. We satisfied some of our desire to drive and our need for speed by running the little boat with the four-horsepower Kohler engine full-speed through ditches and over stumps, exploring the lake, fishing, and getting ready for duck season.

For sure, the shooting was a big part of the hunting, too. Much more for me then than now. Teen-aged boys get blood in their eyes for a while. But shooting a shotgun or a rifle, knowing it was dangerous if mishandled, seeing what it could do and what I could do with it—all of that helped channel those adolescent energies and needs for excitement that seemed almost beyond control for a while.

Still, Dad made sure I understood that killing was not an end in itself.

One day Elton Drysdale, Dad, Sonny Cochran's son Joe, and I were hunting at Reelfoot Lake near the Burnt Woods. It was a bitter day, gray and spitting snow, temperatures never rising above the lower twenties.

Some mallards came in and we knocked down three. We picked up two, but one had fallen in some sawgrass

behind us and we could not find it. After the others finally quit looking, figuring the duck had swum off or simply could not be found, I kept looking. I couldn't stand
to think that the duck might be lying in the grass.

Dad had taught me from the start, "We don't just kill
things. Whatever we shoot, we eat. Or share it with
someone who will eat it." When we killed more than we
could eat, Dad often shared the game with poor folks
who had trouble affording meat.

Like other kids, I watched plenty of movie and television killings. When I hunted, however, I saw that the
dead could not reappear in the next show. Sonny and
Dad made sure I understood that what we saw on television was unreal, that death was real, and that guns
were dangerous. "All it takes is one mistake," Dad said.
"Be careless one time and someone can die."

Many don't understand the "Southern gun culture."
Certainly some who own guns seem to think differently
than Dad did and I do. But what confuses me most is the
"urban gun culture." A city friend gave me some clues,
though. He told me his son, who has never hunted, is
fascinated by and strongly attracted to guns. Many children are. Many of us, especially teenagers, are attracted
to that which we don't understand, to the unknown.

* * *

I would tag along with the Cochrans as they guided
hunters on Reelfoot Lake and Sonny constantly taught
me. He taught hunting skills, like how to blow the duck
call he made for me. "Deeper, down in your throat.
Grunt into it. Grunt."

When to call and when to be quiet. "Most folks call

too much. They talk too much to the ducks. When ducks get in close, don't call much. Just a little chatter or a few quacks."

How to go after cripples, so they didn't get away. "Get between the duck and the refuge. Then work 'em from the refuge back toward the blind."

How to work a black Lab. "You got to be patient. Dogs are like boys—it takes 'em a while to catch on," he'd smile. "But once they do, they're okay."

How to stay warm in the boat. "Put your hand back over the motor's exhaust and you've got your own little heater."

Sonny taught me life lessons, too. Like tending to others' needs before your own. At the start of the hunt, he made sure everyone else was settled in the blind and had their guns loaded first. He lit the charcoal fire for the other hunters in the blind before he even started fooling with the one on our end. At the end of the hunt, he'd send the others to the warm restaurant, while we'd finish putting up the boats.

He taught me to prepare for the next day. We'd fill the engines with gas and check the oil. We'd make sure we were ready, and we'd make sure the people he was guiding the next day knew where to meet us and when.

I learned to look ahead and anticipate. Sonny would watch the clouds and the sunset and the skies. He'd note the wind and watch the weather. "Front coming, Roy. Be some new ducks with it." Then he'd smile, "Better take plenty of shells tomorrow."

He taught me to be careful—and I listened to his advice, even though when Mom told me the same thing it was enough to provoke teenage rebellion. "Make sure somebody knows where you're going on the lake," he warned me. "And when you'll be back. I let my boat get away from the blind one time right before duck season. Too cold to swim after it. I liked to have froze before someone came looking for me. Would have froze if they'd not known I was on the lake."

* * *

More important than anything else were the friendships. The friends with whom we hunted were and are some of my dearest friends.

As I write this, I am looking at a gun cabinet with guns and duck calls all in view. Nancy had trouble at first understanding why I wanted the gun cabinet in my library.

But when I look at the cabinet, I see the 20-gauge Remington that belonged to the grandfather for whom I was named and who died before I was born. I see the Remington 870 pump I "borrowed" from Dad when I thought I was big enough to step up from the 20 to a 12-gauge. There also are the 12-gauge and the 20-gauge Remington Model 1100s Dad bought to replace the guns I took from him. There is the Mossberg .22 rifle my older brother gave me on my thirteenth birthday, which Dad had given him and Uncle Dean had given Dad.

I also see the Reelfoot Lake duck call my teacher Sonny Cochran, a champion call maker, made for me. Next to it are the two little duck calls another friend handed to my twin boys when they were four, and put me in the position of having to take the calls away from the boys or buy them. I decided my sons' calling would be less painful than their squalling.

Those guns and calls remind me of my friends, my teachers, my family, my loved ones. They remind me of a lot of wonderful times. Times when love surrounded me.

Elton Drysdale, the carpenter who rubbed my cold feet and treated me like the son he never had, is gone now. And has been for a long, long time.

Gone five hunting seasons is Sonny Cochran, the guide who taught me to duck hunt and treated me like another son.

And gone is my father, who more than anyone taught me how to hunt and how to live.

They are all gone, but I still find them with me. Each time I go out to hunt again.

THREE

Teams and Dreams

I was a small boy, smaller than almost all the kids my age. I was slow, too, slower than all my friends. The only thing large about me slowed me down—my feet.

When I was so small I couldn't ride a bicycle, I walked with the bigger boys to the baseball field to start playing. To get us out of his way, the coach sent another boy and me to a corner of the outfield. He didn't bother to give us a ball, so we threw dirt clods to each other and learned to catch them with our gloves held out to the side so less dust got in our eyes.

When kids organized neighborhood games, I was picked last. Or not at all. If we had an odd number, after the team captains chose everyone else they would tell me to wait until somebody else showed up to "make the sides even." The games often ended before my waiting did.

In football, I was too slow to run and not big enough to block, as likely to get in the way of my own team as the opposing team. In basketball, if my teammates by mistake or miracle threw me the ball, the other team swarmed me and often stole it away. In baseball, no one wanted me to be an automatic out and cost them an at bat. Even if I got to play, a bigger teammate often would bat for me or at least take my third strike, especially if the game was close.

I loved it when there weren't enough kids to make two teams, because then I usually got to play. Just being chosen for a team was a victory. But even in my own driveway on my goal with my own basketball, bigger kids frequently would not let me play.

I still remember the day I confronted an older boy when he told me I could not play. When I insisted I play, Kenneth knocked me down. I got up and walked back on the court (my own driveway) and he pushed me down again. When I walked onto the court yet again, he yelled names at me and began spitting in my face until I finally backed up. His behavior brought Mother out, which may have been the only way my humiliation could have grown.

* * *

But then there was Mike. Mike Harris was a tall, thin boy, so tall and thin that his arms and elbows were like long knives. Looks were not nearly so important as skills though, and in pick-up games Mike was often a team captain. Mike was about three years older than I was, and for some reason he liked me. When the other kids would say, "Let Roy sit out," Mike would go ahead and

choose me—with his last pick, of course, but still he
chose me.

When Mike picked me for his team, he would encour-
age me. "You can do it!" he'd say. And sometimes, with
his confidence in me, I could.

Playing baseball, I'd run as hard as I could, chasing
flyballs, diving, and sometimes catching them—for
Mike. I'd swing and sometimes connect and then run as
fast as I could to first, occasionally beating the throw—
for Mike. In basketball, I'd throw myself to the concrete
for loose balls—for Mike. In football, trying to protect
quarterback Mike, I'd get in the way of the bigger kids
on the other team, making them knock me down.
Because Mike believed in me, I began to believe in
myself. And I played my heart out for him.

I look back with gratitude, and wonder why he
picked me. Maybe he knew what it was like to be an out-
sider. Maybe he was just a gracious person. I'd ask him
now, but before he finished high school a car wreck
killed him.

* * *

Then there was Jimmy Travis. I didn't play much with
Jimmy because he was too much older and better. But
one afternoon when I was about ten, I wound up at his
house. I don't know where the other kids were, but if
they'd been around Jimmy wouldn't have asked me to
play football with him. Truth to tell, our playing football
didn't last long that day because he was so fast and agile
that he could run around me too easily, and he got
bored. So he decided to teach me to tackle.

"Put your head down," he urged me, "and tackle with

your shoulders. Run your shoulders through the runner, and wrap him up with your arms." But that hurt. With no helmet, no pads, and him so much bigger and stronger, it hurt a lot.

Still, Jimmy insisted. "You can do it. I'll run slow." And he did, at first. And when I grabbed him, he fell. "Way to go!" he yelled, though my ears were only inches from his mouth as we lay on the ground, my arms still around his leg. "Way to go! That was good. Now let's do it again!"

Buoyed by his praise, I got up and prepared to tackle him again. Again he ran slowly and again I brought him down. Then again. And again. He came faster and harder, driving his knees into me. But with his encouragement and cooperation, I'd drive my shoulders into his knees and take him down. Often his knees crashed into my bare head or face. A couple of times we waited for my bloody lips and tears to dry. But again and again we did it, until I knew what to do and how to do it and, most importantly, until I was no longer afraid.

Jimmy's words of praise brought me so much more pleasure than his knees brought pain. So we ran across his front yard time and again, until well past dark.

I don't think I ever played with Jimmy again. He was such a fine athlete that he became an excellent quarterback—in fact, a star. But after that afternoon, every time I saw him I remembered his teaching me how to tackle, to stick my head in there and to hold on and be tough. I never forgot and I was always grateful. I wish I had told him how much he encouraged and helped me. I especially wished I had told him after I learned that he had committed suicide.

* * *

In baseball, it was Tommy Bradberry. Tommy was five years older, a high school hero, and the brother of one of my best friends. One day when I was at their house, as I usually was on summer mornings, he decided to teach me how to catch ground balls. "If you're going to play second base, you've got to catch grounders. And you can't miss them. If you can get to them, you've got to catch them. Understand?" I nodded.

"Get down on them. Get your glove down on the ground," he stressed, bending over and putting his own glove into the grass to show me. "Not getting your glove down is how you miss most of them. Another thing," and he looked me in the eyes, "get in front of the ball. Right in front of it. Don't be afraid of it. Use your body to help stop it."

That did not sound like fun. Who wanted to catch a ball in the chest? But he insisted: "You've got to want to stop the ball more than you want to not get hurt. Got to. Got to. Got to!"

Tommy hit some soft grounders to me—his family's garage was at my back and it stopped the balls I missed. He didn't hit the first ones too fast, and I caught most of them. He bragged on me, then hit some more and hit them harder. He encouraged me, bragged on me some more, fussed at me when I showed my fear of the ball.

Pretty soon I preferred getting hit to letting him down by letting a ball by. And some of the balls did bounce into my body and face. But we were determined that I'd learn how to stop the grounders. And I did. I learned to get my glove down and to get in front of the ball. I learned I wanted to stop the ball more than I wanted to protect myself. And I learned a fundamental lesson: You have to want to win more than you fear pain.

Tommy inspired me. When he joined the Navy and went to Vietnam, I missed him. I sure was glad when he finally came back.

* * *

When I finally got to junior high, at least I got to play. Our school was too small to cut any kids from teams, so everyone who wanted to play made the team. The eighth-grade football coaches started the first practice by timing all of us in the forty-yard dash. Of all the kids, big and fat, short and small, only one other was as slow as I was. Since I was too slow to play in the backfield, the coach put me at center where I wouldn't have to run much. When our coaches encouraged us to be tough, I was as tough as I could be. When they urged us to hit hard, I hit as hard as I could. And when Coach Cheatham bragged on me, I was ready to block a truck for him.

Our team won a couple of games but lost twice as many. At the end of the season, the coach told me I'd get better if I kept trying hard. I played that morsel of encouragement in my head time and again and again.

* * *

By the next fall my father forbade me to play football. ("Too dangerous," he said, easing the blow by giving me a motorcycle. Yes, a motorcycle.) So I focused on basketball, where as a ninth-grader, I was the twenty-fifth fastest of the twenty-five boys on the team. My slowness was repeatedly drilled into me—literally, because the coach used "elimination" drills. Each time we did the drill, the fastest boy or two got to rest, and the others had to do it again. And again. And again. This meant, of course, that not one other player got to run, slide, dribble, or hurt more than I did. In practice, that is. With twenty-five boys on the team, I was fifth team. No game uniform for me. Even Mike Hilliard, the team's student manager, tried to show me how to run faster. He seemed to be wasting his time. But Mike worked with me on building up my speed, and he too became my teacher. I wish I'd thanked him more, also, for he too died in a car wreck.

Eventually, I grew a little. My sophomore year, I finally got one of the fifteen home suits and got to sit on the bench during home games. My junior year I also got one of the twelve road uniforms and finally lettered. But I sat out most of those games on the bench. Still, I wasn't as bad as I had been.

The summer before my senior year, I went to a basketball camp, won a shooting contest, finally gained a little confidence. That fall before practice began, I got up early in the mornings before school and ran to and from the same park I had walked to as a child to catch dirt clods in the outfield. The two miles of running were more than I had ever done and more than I thought my teammates were doing. I'd not forgotten I had been the slowest player on our team. I wanted to do more than anyone else, since I had farther to go.

By now I was about six feet tall and considerably quicker. Now when we ran sprints, I often led the team. To be sure, other guys could beat me if they wanted to, but they rarely wanted to enough. I finally made the starting five.

Two of my happiest memories are from two games

my senior year in high school. Early in the season, a team had beaten us by twenty points on our own home court, but when we played them again, it was another story. We had worked like heck through the season and had come to believe we could beat them. In a large upset, on their court, we won by a single point.

Then a much larger school came to play us again. They had blown us out by more than thirty points at their gymnasium. Their talented college-bound athletes were expecting more easy pickings. But we beat them by about ten—a forty point turn-around. We were stunned by our success that night. And the sweetness of that victory has hardly dimmed through the years.

Our coach that year, Larry Carter, had encouraged me and tried to get me to believe in myself. At the end of the season, he told me I should try out for the team at the nearby college. I hadn't even thought about that, especially because one night the college recruiter had seen me arch a shot so high that the ball struck a light.

But because Coach Carter encouraged me, I tried out for the junior varsity basketball team. I barely made it, but I did. I was a third-team point guard again, mostly riding the bench, but at least I was on the team that won sixteen and lost only four. The next year, I didn't make the team again and that ended my collegiate career in this country. After graduation, I played in Scotland for another successful university team and I was selected for the Scottish Universities All-Stars. I had never been an all-star before, not even in Little League, and I've sure never been one since. I laugh to think that I had to leave our country to become one. Still, Coach Carter's encouragement had followed me across the Atlantic.

* * *

"Daddy, you promised," the coach-pitch rookies reminded me, "to take us to our first Major League game *this year*."

The next tickets available in St. Louis were "standing room only" on a school day a month later. But I'd promised.

On game day I told two second-grade teachers I was taking my twins "on a field trip to study physics and physiology, as well as geography and history." Ms. Amy laughed and Mrs. Brandy grinned, "Your sons said you were taking them to *The Game*."

The boys climbed in the backseat of the Cardinal red pickup and began:

"Daddy, sir, do you think Mark McGwire will hit number 62 tonight?"

"He could, Rick."

"But do you think he will, Daddy, sir?"

"I think it is possible, but not probable. Do you understand the difference between 'possible' and 'probable'?"

John volunteered:

"One means he could and the other means he will?"

"That's close."

"But Daddy," the sons of two lawyers continued the cross-examination, "do you think he *will*?"

"Honestly, son, I don't. Even McGwire only averages a home run about every third game." Now I knew how Scrooge felt in September.

At Paducah, we picked up a third-grader named Ann and her preacher dad. My son immediately asked my minister friend," Greg, do you think McGwire will hit number 62 tonight?"

"Ab-so-lutely!" the man of faith replied. "I think tonight is *The Night*!"

So much for holding down expectations and disappointment.

After five hours and six stops, we walked from the truck to the stadium. Stop seven was the first souvenir stand. It was a little after 4:00 p.m., just three hours until game time.

We staked a claim on the second level, near the left-field line, behind the last row of seats. We stood next to a principal perched on a stool who admitted leaving school early also—and she lived in St. Louis.

During the National Anthem, Rick put his new Cardinals hat over his chest. John reverently stared at his new Cardinals flag. Fifty thousand listened to the singer, but we helped her.

The Cubs pitcher mowed down the first eleven Cards. Then Mark McGwire again walked to the plate.

Camera flashes made the stadium look like a giant sparkler. Everyone who could speak, screamed. Everyone who could stand, stood. I lifted John and Rick to a railing, then they bent their knees so those behind could see, too.

McGwire stroked the first pitch, a line drive landing below but near us and just inside the yellow foul pole: number 62.

I tried to keep the boys from jumping off the railing onto someone's head. The stadium went nuts. And stayed there. Even the Cubs fans applauded and shouted.

The next time McGwire came up, the Cubs intentionally walked him. We all booed. Then Lankford launched a three-run homer. Gant followed with another blast.

Rick shouted to his brother over the roar, "Can you believe it? Two home runs in a row *and* number 62!"

John yelled back, "This is definitely one of the greatest days in baseball history!"

The Cardinals won 6-to-3.

But much of the evening's wonder is not in the box score nor will it be in the record books.

No one wanted to keep McGwire from getting number 62 more than the teammates of Sammy Sosa who had 58. Plus, the Cubs were battling for the playoffs. The competition was intense.

And yet when McGwire homered, each Cubs infielder congratulated McGwire. The third baseman and the catcher even hugged him. Outfielder Sosa ran in to embrace McGwire as well.

When McGwire batted, fans cheered. But when McGwire's rival came to bat, the crowd cheered Sosa, too.

When Cubs pitchers walked McGwire, fans booed. But when a Cardinal pitcher threw Sosa a ball, much less a base-on-balls, Cardinals fans booed their own hurlers, also.

The fans were of one mind. They were for the game's two best home run hitters doing their best. They were fans of The Game. And of those who play. For one night, at least, competition did not mean being against someone, but rather being for everyone. The Game was about believing and about overcoming, no matter how insurmountable the challenge seemed.

Amazing in itself was the capacity crowd getting along. So many standing could have been selfish and shoving instead of caring and cooperative. Sosa and McGwire set the tone. As did Roger Maris' children, all of whom were gracious to McGwire. Just their being there was an act of conciliation with the man competing with their late father. McGwire rightly and repeatedly expressed respect for them and their late father.

The evening scarcely contained the excitement and even ecstasy of excellence exemplified. Children's dreams came true. And new dreams were born.

At the end of the night, my son John sighed, "This has been a glorious evening...."

He was right. And not just for the reasons in the record books.

FOUR

Growing Up with the Flag

*T*he courthouse in Dawson, Georgia, stands near the spot where a gun factory once stood that served the Confederate States of America. The courthouse is brick and Gothic and garish. Round turrets soar from the corners of the building, and the clock tower rises high above it all.

In the wall of a porch, just above and to the right of the Royal Crown Cola thermometer, a marble slab declares: Terrell County Court House—Erected 1892.

On another porch is a shoeshine stand where the court house janitor, a prisoner from the jail next door, uses a white rag and black hands to polish black and brown shoes worn by white men.

Inside the dark lobby, a single, gray, square, wooden pillar rises from the gray linoleum to support the upstairs court room. Next to the pillar stands an old gray metal water fountain. Attached to the pillar above the fountain is a Dixie cup dispenser. The dispenser appeared after the 1964 Civil Rights Act mandated permission for blacks to use the fountain.

The first time I saw the courthouse was in July 1977. A child's red, white, and blue toy flag had been stuck behind the cup dispenser, its thirty-two inch, gold-tipped stick protruding below the Dixie cups, the cloth drooping beside them. It was just like the Confederate flags I had gotten at Fort Donelson and Shiloh when I was a boy.

* * *

But even before I ever went to Fort Donelson or Shiloh, I knew about Fort Henry, another Civil War historic site near home. The fort had been on the Tennessee River, near our cabin. The first major Union victory in the western theater had taken place there in February 1862.

When I was four or so, my parents showed me the Minie ball they had found near the ruins. As we would drive by in our boat, I imagined that I was a sentry on the walls of the fort. The Confederate flag stood guard over me.

When I was eight or nine, my mother took me to Fort Donelson, on the Cumberland River. It was only about thirty-five miles from Fort Henry, and was the fort to which the troops from Fort Henry had fled. I learned then that it was at Fort Donelson that U.S. Grant won the nickname that went with his initials when he demanded and received an unconditional surrender. I could not understand why we had given him what he wanted.

For three days the Confederates had won the upper hand, then almost inexplicably the generals decided to surrender. Later, two generals were censured for deserting their responsibilities. Grant captured as many as 15,000 prisoners, 20,000 stands of arms, 48 artillery pieces, 17 heavy guns, 4,000 horses, and a huge quantity of commissary supplies. It was a stunning defeat for our South.

I was told Fort Donelson was the first Confederate fort to suffer the capture of its flag. A century later, when my mother sounded retreat and we headed for home, I carried my souvenir toy Confederate flag safely with me.

Also near our home, thirty-four miles up the Tennessee River from Fort Henry, was Pilot Knob, a hill high above the river. Here Nathan Bedford Forrest, who had refused to surrender at Fort Donelson, had led the battle. By the time Forrest went to Pilot Knob, he had become a general known for leading slashing, dashing, fearless cavalry attacks that destroyed huge numbers of bluebellies, leaving most of our boys unscratched. Mom and Dad told me General Forrest always believed in getting there "fustest with the mostest" (first with the most men).

At Pilot Knob, General Forrest used artillery to take on the Union navy, successfully blockading shipping and disabling and destroying several Union vessels. Then he destroyed the Union supply depot across the Tennessee River at nearby Johnsonville. After the Civil War, he was the first Grand Wizard of the Ku Klux Klan. My Boy Scout district was named for General Forrest.

Each summer at church camp, we hiked to Pilot Knob to picnic in Nathan Bedford Forrest State Park.

The park's concrete and stone building looked like a castle to me then. Names and dates and epigraphs were painted and scratched on almost every rock. Some of the art was beyond the understanding of an unsophisticated fifth-grader, but I did admire a red rectangle with an "X" through it. Over the years I had drawn hundreds of such flags at school, as well as several at home on the nice blank pages in the front and back of the encyclopedias, and once in the dining room on Mother's new wall-paper.

Farther south up the Tennessee River from Pilot Knob was Shiloh, the site of the second bloodiest battle of the Civil War. On the first day of the battle, we mauled the Northern army. On the second day, Grant's reinforcements forced the South to withdraw.

My brother and I went to Shiloh for a reenactment of the battle. Weekend warriors raced across the fields, charging and attacking, falling and feigning death. As soon as one flagbearer began to fall, another soldier would seize the flag and save it from touching the ground. At the souvenir shop, I bought a little gray hat with a stiff brim, one like the cannoneers wore. On its gray felt top was a sticker, an emblem of the flag. My brother and I watched Saturday's victories; we did not stay for Sunday's defeats.

On still another childhood trip to Shiloh, I bought two miniature cannons similar to those I had seen in the law office of Mr. Gallimore, a colleague of Dad's. One of Mr. Gallimore's cannons guarded his office from a table behind his desk. Above the table, covering about twenty-five square feet of wall, was our Confederate flag.

Whenever Dad and I would go by Mr. Gallimore's house to pick him up to go fishing, I always wanted to go inside. Inside was everything this Confederate boy soldier needed—swords for slashing and guns for sharpshooting. Two generals astride their horses beckoned from the mantelpiece, eager to give orders. Generals Robert E. Lee and Stonewall Jackson told Private Herron what to do and he moved them across the battlefield to the edge of the rug. Only reluctantly did I obey the orders to leave my plastic leaders and go with Mr. Gallimore and Dad.

In front of Mr. Gallimore's house flew a Confederate flag like the one in his office. It flew from a pole that seemed as big as the one on the south side of the courthouse, the one that flew the American flag. That American flagpole marked one end zone of our football field—the courthouse lawn; marking the other was a marble statue topped by a Confederate soldier. During breaks, we sat at the base of the statue. Above our heads, carved into the marble, was the flag.

Like Mr. Gallimore, I had ancestors who fought in the war. Because one was an officer, I was told, my sister could have had a free room in Confederate Hall at Peabody College in Nashville. Instead she went to the University of Tennessee campus in our home county. I followed her there. From the campus, I could see Mr. Gallimore's home. The flag was gone by then, though. Mr. Gallimore had died.

* * *

For me, the flag began to lose some of its sacredness

when I joined a service fraternity in college. Wendell Wainwright, our fraternity president, was from Fayette County, near Memphis. Fayette County was one of the poorest and blackest counties in the United States. One book reported at the time that Fayette County was "the third poorest county in America" and about sixty percent black. Wendell was black.

Wendell slowly taught me about his home county and the experiences of blacks there. He explained that even voting was dangerous for African-Americans in Fayette County. He told me about blacks evicted from land they long had sharecropped because they dared register to vote. Wendell shared stories of other African-American farmers, landowners who were denied loans and could not plant crops, because they dared try to vote. He told of a "blacklist" of black registered voters distributed by racist whites to businesses throughout the county. Those black voters soon could not buy anything from anyone anywhere in the county, at least not until blacks started their own businesses. Later, Wendell said, blacks turned the tables and boycotted white merchants who had mistreated their black neighbors.

Wendell also told of men and women who suffered beatings and even death, their attackers too often going unpunished. He told me of jailings followed by injustice in the courts. He told in detail about separate and unequal schools, including the schools Wendell had attended before we went to college together.

Wendell said some of the evicted homeless left the county, but many stayed and found refuge on the few black-owned farms. Some lived at "Tent City," where children and the elderly suffered most from winter's cold in tents and shelters made of boards, cardboard, and rusted tin. As if that were not enough, after a while hostile visitors came to "Tent City." Whites drove by shouting, then shooting. Some especially brave survivors of these struggles told the story in a book called *Our Portion of Hell.*

In the spring of my freshman year, Wendell dared to run for student body president. Soon visitors came. Whites drove by his dorm, shouting. Then someone threw a rock, striking a fraternity brother.

The next year, I won the race that Wendell had lost. He and a classmate named Emmett Edwards were crucial supporters. Emmett was from Tipton County, which borders Fayette County. Near his home, my old hero, Nathan Bedford Forrest, had captured Fort Pillow, a former Confederate fort then held by the Union and manned by about three hundred white troops and about an equal number of blacks, including many former slaves. What the whites in gray did to the blacks in blue has been a controversy ever since. Two-thirds of the blacks, and almost a third of the white unionists, were killed. Some defended the killing as justified by the refusal of the Union troops to surrender until most had died. Others called it "The Fort Pillow Massacre."

* * *

Wendell and Emmett told me that the Confederate flag I had grown up adoring meant something very different to them.

To me, it symbolized my ancestors' courage. To them, it symbolized my ancestors' prejudice.

To me, it had nothing to do with their ancestors. To them, it had everything to do with their ancestors—and their slavery.

To me, it meant freedom from Northern oppression. To them, it meant Southern oppression.

To me, it recalled a proud history. To them, it recalled a painful history.

To me, the flag stood for the South. To them, the flag stood for slavery.

Eventually, I realized that if my ancestors who fought under that flag had been victorious, Wendell and Emmett might have been my chattel instead of my classmates, my property instead of my teachers. They might have picked my cotton, some of which could have gone to make more flags.

* * *

In 1977, when I first saw the flag over the water fountain in the courthouse in Dawson, I thought it must be the Georgia state flag. When no one was looking, I lifted and extended the cloth. The blue and the state seal in the Georgia flag were not there. This was the genuine article, the Rebel battle flag.

As I sat and waited on a bench in the lobby, a small, old, black man in large, old baggy pants, white shirt, wide suspenders and a straw hat came to drink. When he reached for a cup, his hat almost touched the flag. He said he did not mind posing for a photograph, but I knew he did.

A week later, before a white judge in the gray and white courtroom upstairs, the white prosecutors were about to begin the case against five innocent black youths for the murder of a white man. Just before the hearings began, another law student on the defense team and I walked through the black crowd in the lobby.

"Before this case is over," I laughed to my friend as we passed the flag, "someone's going to carry that flag away."

As the hearings began, and after eighteen months of terror for the teenaged black defendants and their families, the prosecutors announced they no longer sought electrocution. Now they simply demanded that the five youngsters spend the rest of their lives in prison.

The hearings stretched over two weeks. The attorneys for the defense, for whom I worked as a law clerk, showed several law enforcement officers to be liars and helped a Methodist minister make himself appear the same—and he may have been. Witnesses exposed the pervasiveness of segregation in Dawson—the illegally segregated public swimming pools, public housing, and public schools with only a handful of the poorest whites. Even, and perhaps especially, the churches were segregated. The segregation did not stop with death, for the graveyards, of course, also were segregated.

Testimony revealed that white policemen in town routinely beat black adults. Some white officers even drove through black neighborhoods throwing hot dogs dipped in arsenic to black children's dogs.

Strict segregation, law-breaking by law enforcement officials, intimidation and violence—these were the context of and the explanation of how so-called "confessions" were obtained from two teenagers. The defense attorneys asked the judge to throw out the two statements white officers had gotten with guns and threats of castration and electrocution.

A former police sergeant testified that he had held the sixteen-year-old defendant as a deputy put a pistol to the bridge of the teen's nose and slowly pulled the trigger. The gun's hammer went back farther and farther and came within a fraction of an inch of splattering the teen's brains on the back window of the patrol car. The deputy had demanded, "Talk, nigger! Where'd you throw those guns?" Terrified, the sixteen-year-old had said he threw them in a pond near his home. Of course, since he had never had the murder weapon or any other firearm, no gun was found in the pond or anywhere else.

The other alleged "confession" occurred after white law enforcement officers took another teenager out of town, put him in a stark, white-walled room, hooked him to a white polygraph machine, and convinced the black youngster that he was about to be electrocuted and that to avoid his own death he had to say he'd committed the murder. The statement then was written and even signed by someone other than the teen defendant, someone who signed the wrong name. When they'd unhooked him from what he thought was an electric chair, he'd refused to repeat the lie.

The attorneys also asked the judge to reject an "eyewitness" identification given by the white storeowner in whose store the killing had taken place. They pointed out that for three days after the shooting the storeowner said he had not recognized the masked men, and then decided that "it might possibly have been" his nearby black neighbors.

The judge announced he would take some time to decide what he would do about the fate of my five friends. Eventually the judge threw out the coerced and false statements by the two teens. Months went by before the prosecution finally dropped the charges against the five innocent youngsters.

* * *

After the hearing, I lingered in the courtroom. When I finally came downstairs to the courthouse lobby, I stopped to get a drink of water. The toy Confederate flag was no longer hanging by the Dixie cup dispenser. I looked around, but only the prisoner-janitor shoeshine man was in sight.

The old black man had put the flag on top of the soft-drink machine while he refilled the Dixie cup dispenser. I asked him whose flag it was. He told me a deputy had placed it there. The same deputy who had placed a pistol to the head of the sixteen-year-old and squeezed the trigger while demanding a confession for a crime the young man did not commit. The prisoner-janitor whispered to me, "I sure do wish somebody'd take it away."

The old black man walked down the hall toward his shoeshine stand. He stopped outside the sheriff's office, looked in, then looked at me and nodded. As the prisoner stood guard, I took the toy flag, pushed it up the left sleeve of my gray coat, and rested the end of the stick in the palm of the hand that carried my briefcase. Then I walked casually out the door.

FIVE

The Old Scout

*W*hen I called Nancy, I did not say, "Gwin Crawford died." Or even, "Granddaddy Crawford died." But simply, "Granddaddy died."

He was not Granddaddy with a surname. He was simply *Granddaddy*.

* * *

He wasn't really my grandfather. Mother's father died before I was born and Dad's father died when I was young, and he took their place.

He wasn't a grandfather just for me. He was that for a long string of boys well before his hair turned white and his shoulders stooped a bit. He had joined the first Boy Scout troop in McKenzie, Tennessee, in 1911 or 1912, only a year or two after the Boy Scout movement started in America. He soon became a Scout leader. Except for a few years during World War I and while he worked away from home, he was a Scout leader all his adult life.

After his wife died and he retired in 1961, he moved the twenty miles from McKenzie to Dresden to live with one of his three daughters. I was seven years old. There he became a Scout leader for many more of us. He may have worked with as many as 2,000 Scouts. I was one. Only my parents impacted me more.

*   *   *

"What did Mr. Crawford do?" asked the reporter at the obituary desk of *The Commercial Appeal* newspaper.

It would have been easier to tell the reporter what Granddaddy did not do. Flour mill maintenance man. TVA carpenter and construction worker on a floating piledriver. World War I Navy sailing instructor. River pilot. Boat builder. But he always told people he was a millwright.

The night before we buried him, I learned he'd also owned and operated a restaurant, a tin and sheet metal shop, and a feed mill. Years later I found out he also had been a dental technician and manufactured dentures, operated an ice delivery wagon, and managed the local ice house.

All these public jobs were exactly that: jobs, ways to make a living. But his calling was teaching young people, mostly his Boy Scouts. Admittedly, his formal education was sparse by today's standards. His handwriting was illegible and his spelling was creative, with innovations such as "gawn" for "gone" and omitting a "t" in his daughter Patty's name. I've experienced more than

my share of formal education, but my most important
teacher was this college drop-out who bounced from job
to job.

* * *

I thought I'd started most everyone calling him
"Granddaddy." His real grandson Gwin and I were
hanging out with him in his dusty, dirt-floored shop
crammed full of wood-working tools and a boat or two.
We were not even as tall as the wood stove or work
bench. Gwin called him Granddaddy, so as a little boy
joke, I started doing the same. But the name fit—and
stuck.

Granddaddy gave me a name, too. That started with
the first long sailboat trip he took me on. The summer
after Gwin and I finished third grade, he took us for a
week on the Tennessee River. One morning as we were
breaking camp, I was carrying a Coleman gas stove
down a steep hill to the boat. I tripped on a root and
stumbled into the river. I dropped the stove so I didn't
take it with me. Soon Granddaddy announced, "I guess
I'm going to have to call you 'Roy with the Two Left
Feet.'"

He did then and plenty of other times, when I fell into
the lake or toppled to the ground. There were lots of
those times, because after that trip went pretty well
(after all, I had not ruined his camp stove), he took me to
raise.

* * *

Gwin's father and Granddaddy decided they wanted
a place on Kentucky Lake, the part of the Tennessee

River nearest our home. Before long, near the top of a steep hill a stone's throw above the lake, in a clearing shadowed by tall trees, we were building "The Cabin."

At age ten, Gwin and I considered ourselves construction engineers and experienced builders. After all, we'd been in Granddaddy's shop ever since he moved to Dresden. We'd measured, sawed, nailed, even painted. To be sure, most of the wood scraps became battleships, swords, or other devices intended to maim enemies, but usually wielded on unsuspecting friends. Now, Granddaddy decided, it was time for us to make something more useful. So we did.

Gwin and I learned to carry cement blocks, mix mortar, put up studs, hang wallboard, roll roofing, put down shingles, and squirm in the attic laying fiberglass insulation. Granddaddy caught many of our mistakes and kept us from doing too much damage, either to the building or to ourselves, until he could teach us to do things right.

"Roy, you just think that nail's jumping when you swing at it. Hit it, hit it hard and straight." "That knot is the toughest piece of the wood; you might move your nail over a little." "If you'll keep some pressure on that board, it won't bite your saw." "If you get that plumb line tight, real tight, then you can pop it. . . . Don't break my string, though!" "It's easier to do it right the first time than to have to tear it out and do it again."

He was pushy but patient. There was a right way to do things—Granddaddy's way—and a wrong way. He seemed to know everything. And how to do everything.

When he'd pushed us all that knot-headed little boys could be pushed, he would pay for our labor by teaching us how to motorboat, sail, navigate by the stars, swim like fish, water ski, shoot bows and arrows, and camp.

By the winter, we were enjoying The Cabin. It had a nine-bed bunkroom for us kids, two bedrooms for adults, a den, bathroom, kitchen and big screened-in porch. Two huge windows provided ventilation in the summer and a wood-burning Franklin stove gave heat in the winter. It was the grandest place on earth.

* * *

The next winter Granddaddy took Gwin and me on a cold Thanksgiving weekend to The Cabin. Saturday morning Gwin and I went down to the lake while Granddaddy worked at the cabin. Gwin saw a couple of duck hunters capsize in the middle of the lake. Granddaddy had taught us how to operate his sailboat and the small outboard on it, so Gwin and I went and picked up the freezing men.

Granddaddy hadn't heard their cries for help and was surprised to see us all walk in, the two men soaked and shivering. He insisted they take warm showers and gave them hot coffee and dry clothes. Before long they went home, none the worse for their trial.

If Granddaddy bragged on us, either then or later, I don't recall it. All he told the local newspaper was, "There wasn't another person on that area of the lake. It's just a good thing the boys decided to go down to the beach and their boat."

That was it. And that was all there should have been. He'd taught us to handle that boat. We just did what he taught us. Even though we too often acted like eleven-year-old boys, he knew we could act responsibly. On the water he insisted upon it. This time we were glad that he had.

Now, just because Granddaddy didn't waste breath bragging did not mean he didn't talk to us about the day's events. In fact, he talked a lot about what had happened, gave his opinion on why the canoe capsized, and stressed again the dangers of winter boating. He lectured us on how to avoid the same predicament—and what to do if we didn't. He was not much of a bragger. But he was, as ever, a teacher.

* * *

His best teaching, though, came not from his mouth but from his example.

I never saw him take a drink.

He had quit smoking a half-century earlier when he started working with Scouts, telling his boys if they wouldn't smoke, he would stop. He told us, time and again, if you saved the money that two packs of cigarettes a day cost, you could buy a nice house by the time you were a certain age. He had the figures all worked out. I don't recall the exact numbers, but few of us forgot the lesson.

I never heard him curse. Not once. The closest he came was "Sam Hale." And, of course, quite a few times I heard, and deserved to hear, "Dadburn your time, Roy!"

I don't remember ever hearing him raise his voice in anger. Oh, he got a little louder when he was exasperated and at times we exasperated even him. But never did he speak angrily to or shout at me.

In almost four decades, his son-in-law never heard

him say one hard word against anybody. Nor did I.

Unless there was a dangerous situation, he didn't give orders or commands. Instead, he would request or suggest, starting with words like "Wouldn't you like to . . . ?" "How would you like to . . . ?" "Wouldn't it be better . . . ?" His Scouts remembered him not as a commander or dictator, but as a leader.

* * *

For almost seventy-five years, Granddaddy raised children. For almost three-quarters of a century, he was a Scout leader. He taught us Scouts how to make everything we needed and much of what we wanted. He showed us how to work on wood and metal, first with his hand tools and then, eventually, with his power tools. He taught us to build, repair, take care of, and operate boats. He taught us to swim, sail, ski. He taught us the rules of the river. He taught us to build a fire with only two matches, with no matches and only steel and flint, and with friction alone. He taught us to cook over that same fire, to dry ourselves and keep warm by it, to make sure it didn't die during the night, and to start a new fire from its coals. He taught us to camp, how to survive on little or nothing in the woods, and how, if we had a little something, we could feast and live like kings. He taught us more ways to do more things with a rope, and more ways to knot that rope, than the Scout Handbook even dreamed. He taught us how to enjoy our lives and save others' lives. Three decades later, I still hear him teaching during the dozens of trips we took. In fact, today I still pay attention to his advice, maybe more now even than then.

"Roy, you dove in and came up with mud on your head. You dive without knowing what's under the surface and some day you're gonna find a stump."

"Always, always swim with a buddy. You never know when you might get a cramp or need help."

"Pick up your trash and anybody else's, too, so you leave a place nicer than you found it. That way everybody's better off."

When we were intimidated by anything, from the weather to doing something new, he always had a response.

"A little water can't hurt you. I've never seen any germs in rain."

"Go ahead and try. I'll help you—but I'm not going to do it for you—you wouldn't learn anything if I did."

Gold did not rule Granddad, but the golden rule did. And if we didn't learn it or sometimes forget it, it's not because we weren't taught. Nor was it because we lacked an example.

* * *

Granddaddy often said, "I never worked with a boy in Scouting that went to prison." I figured he was warning us to straighten up so we didn't break his record and get a record. Occasionally he would point out that one youngster almost went to prison. At least six dozen of us who heard him say that thought we were that one boy. I just couldn't figure out why more of my friends didn't almost go with me, since most of our mischief was collective. For example, at Scout camp it was a group of us who, with a hunting knife, gave the long-haired boy a haircut, which we thought he needed, but cut his head, which the doctor thought needed stitches.

Now, he took delight in *some* misbehavior. He even told his three daughters bedtime stories of pranks his boys pulled. Granddad enjoyed teaching skills and suggesting pranks so youngsters could enjoy enough good mischief to avoid serious trouble.

Granddaddy was right when he said his youngsters did not go to prison. Because he took boys and made men. He took girls and made women. He taught his granddaughters and other girls to swim, sail, and camp. He took his grandson and me and others and helped us achieve Scouting's highest rank. In one patrol alone at one time he had seven Eagle Scouts—and the other youngster achieved Life, the next highest rank. Our Dresden troop had six Eagles at one camp. With his help, literally dozens and perhaps hundreds of his boys became Eagle Scouts.

He stressed cooperation instead of competition. But he also knew competition made us better. And if there was going to be competition, he wanted his boys to win. "No sense competing if you're not going to do your best," he'd remind us. And he figured our best, together with his best, ought to be good enough to win. One time his troop competed with 150 troops and took seven of the ten first prizes. The other three first prizes went to the other two McKenzie troops that competed with his youngsters and learned from him, too.

* * *

In 1972 when he was seventy-six, an area newspaper did a story on him, calling him "An Old Scout." I'm sure he grimaced at the "old," for the article reported

Granddad could not just go downtown and sit around, swapping knives and talking with his contemporaries. Granddaddy, instead, shared his life's motto with the reporter:

"I've got to be doing something. I've got to move out. . . . I'd rather be with young people helping them learn something than with old people."

At the age of eighty-one he was awarded the Silver Beaver Award, one of the highest honors in Scouting. Granddaddy explained to me the award usually went to donors, not doers. In 1985 our hometown paper did a story on him. The writer observed that he could have posed as the grandfatherly ideal in a Norman Rockwell painting, but he never would sit still long enough.

At age 89 he maintained that his secret for staying young was "Never sit down! You know, people retire and just sit down. Once they sit down, that's all you ever hear of them. I haven't sat down yet." To prove his point, he noted that in the summer of that, his 89th year, he attended Camp Mack Morris as a Scout leader for the eighteenth consecutive year, a string begun when he took his grandson and a bunch of us there.

By the time he turned ninety, he estimated he had worked with more than 2,000 Boy Scouts. That year, friends and former Scouts organized "Gwin Crawford Day." A hundred Scouts and friends came from every region of the country and from as far away as Hawaii to honor him and celebrate his life.

Other former Scouts wrote letters. One referred to Granddad's having taught him and his Depression-era Scouts how to make their own tents and packs and equipment, since they could not afford to buy any of those things. The former Scout wrote, "You taught us a feeling of independence that gave us confidence and has carried through all these years. When I am improvising something out of nothing I think how we used to 'make do' regardless of what we had available. Things such as those are not taught in school and are not available to everyone."

Another summarized the shared feelings of all who gathered and many who could not: "Gwin Crawford must have been born to love boys—boys of all ages."

* * *

A few months before he passed, Granddaddy asked his grandson Gwin as they rode in his truck, "Which do you think is going to wear out first—me or this old truck?"

Near the end, Granddaddy kept saying that if he could walk he could get his strength back. His son-in-law Joe pointed out that he could not even stand up, much less walk. Granddaddy told Joe that if he got on one side and his grandson Gwin got on the other, it would look like he was walking. So down the hall of the nursing home they and Granddaddy would "walk." Joe instructed Granddaddy's great-granddaughter Martha to follow them with the wheelchair, and if Granddaddy fell, "Scoop him up!"

His last week, Granddaddy was so weak he could barely suck his straw. He complained that they were not giving him enough exercise.

Granddaddy died in 1987. His family asked me to conduct his funeral. I had never led a funeral service. He probably chuckled at my discomfort. After all, he was always calling on us to do new things, teaching us to do different things. Even in death, he pushed and taught me one last time.

At the service, the room was filled with his boys. They ranged from teenagers he'd worked with shortly before his death to eighty-something-year-olds he'd led when he was barely older than they were. They had gone with him to Scout camps and camporees, over to Reelfoot Lake, up and down the Tennessee River, to the Smoky Mountains and Washington, D.C. He had also taken them through the ranks of Scouting: Tenderfoot, Second Class, First Class, Star, Life, even and especially Eagle. He had taken them as his boys, and they had become their own men.

But as I looked at the moist-eyed men, it was clear that once you were one of Granddaddy's boys, you were *always* his boy.

* * *

Granddaddy's earthly life ended on Good Friday and we buried him on Easter Sunday. One of his boys said it seemed right to bury his body on Easter: knowing Granddaddy, he might just decide to sit up and be resurrected. And we did about half expect him to get up and go. That's how he was for ninety years.

But it also was an ironic time for Granddaddy to depart. For he did not spend much time in church buildings. He went to church only for funerals, weddings, or Eagle ceremonies. One of his Scouts even said, "He's the most Christian atheist I know."

But Granddaddy was not an atheist. Nor was he even anti-church. The week he died his family received from the Cumberland Presbyterian Church of McKenzie a statement of Granddaddy's recent financial contributions. Unbeknownst to even his own family, he'd given to that church all his life. No, Granddad was not an atheist. He just walked the walk a lot more than he talked the talk. In fact, he was simply the quietest Christian I've known.

When I think of Granddaddy, I recall the words from the third chapter of First John: "Little children, let us not love in word or speech, but in deed and in truth" (RSV).

SIX

The Last Harvest

$\mathcal{I}$ grew up knowing that something about the land was sacred.

I knew because my father loved to go to the farm every chance he got. Dad was at peace, even joyful, at the farm, whether taking care of the cattle, driving the tractor, checking the crops, or just being there.

I could hear the sacred in the respectful, even reverent way that Dad, his father, and Uncle Dean talked about their farms.

I could see the sacredness in Grandmother's faithfulness. Even when she was in her seventies, even during the hottest summer months, she would get in the fields with another youngster and me and help clear saplings and trees.

Mother explained that one of my ancestors had been

the first non-Native American to settle in our county, even before people were supposed to reside here. She said we had been farming here since he arrived in 1819. He had come to claim and settle on land that would support his family and let them build their lives. He and the generations since had lived on and from this land, died on and been buried in it.

I suppose Dad was the first in a long line not to make his living primarily from the land. Still, he did what he had to do to make a living, then returned to the farm every day he could.   And took me with him every time I would go.

When I was tiny, he put me on the front of the seat of the big, red Farmall 400 International Harvester tractor and reached around me to shift and steer. When I was a little bigger, he taught me how to drive the tractor myself. And put me to work mowing or bush hogging, doing something that I couldn't mess up too badly.

Eventually Dad joined in a partnership with some neighbors named Capps. We were partners in a few head of Hereford beef cattle, and the Capps family also started cropping our ground. The story of the Capps family brings home the sacredness of the land again and again.

* * *

Pappy John Capps was the patriarch of the family that farmed our land when my father died and my brother moved away. His skin was dark from decades in the fields. His hair was silver except for where it was white. He did not hear as well as he once had, but he carried himself erect still.

Pappy John lived in Weakley County, Tennessee for more than eighty years, most of them in a log house. Weather-boarded on the outside, daubed and sealed on the inside, the walls were eight to ten inches thick and made of poplar logs. "Hewed those logs out. Not sawed out, hewed out with a broadax," he would tell you.

He was not sure how many generations of his family had farmed, but he did not remember any that did not. He helped his father on the farm until he married in his twenties and began farming for himself, though he and his father helped each other out. "I was never more than half a mile from him," he would say. His two sons in turn helped him on the farm until they married.

In 1946, son Billy married Sarah Adams of nearby Sharon, Tennessee. She worked for a year in a factory, then a year in a shoe store. Mainly though, she raised their two children and worked on the land that she and Billy had begun to farm. When they had the last harvest, she was fifty-nine and her hair was gray and her once-strong voice was less firm than it used to be. She lived in a brick home that her brother built for her and Billy. Her daughter Brenda lived nearby; her son Rick lived just up the road.

Rick Capps was thirty-eight and had the look of a farmer: broad shoulders, bulky arms, big hands. He was quick to look you in the eye. He wrote poetry, painted, preached occasionally, and studied the Bible continually. He graduated from the county's University of Tennessee campus in 1971 and taught English in two nearby towns. He got his master's degree in education, got married, started a family.

In 1973, Rick bought a house within sight of his parents' home and started farming full-time. "I had been on the farm all my life," he says. "I was taught farming growing up and farming has always been a part of me and I have always been a part of it."

In 1975, Rick and his father Billy decided to form a partnership and farm on a larger scale. They did not buy more land, they cropped on shares. Part of the land they farmed belonged to my family.

To farm the additional land, they went to a tractor dealer, picked out a brand-new John Deere 4020, and took it home. But it was not big enough after all, so they bought another. Then they bought a disc, a plow, a ripper, a planter, a used truck for hauling grain, a spray rig, and a John Deere 4400 combine.

Rick, Bill, and Pappy John shared the equipment to work the 750 acres they now were farming. They also shared the debt. And then they shared the drought.

"In 1980 or so, it just got harder and harder to keep your head above water," says Rick. "Inflation got higher and interest rates got higher and crop prices were down. Like all farmers always do, we kept thinking that next year would be better, this was just a bad one, we'll just cut back a bit and work a little harder and next year will be better." They cut back on fertilizer that year, and repairs and maintenance on their equipment.

Over the next two years, Pappy John began to "taper," as they say. Billy had to quit his second job as a railroad switchman in Fulton, Kentucky, because the fifty-mile commute made it hard to devote the necessary time to the farm. Then Billy's cancer came, and he had to have his larynx removed. Then came 1983, the year the Capps call the real cruncher.

Pappy John said he had seen only two or three

droughts like it. Rick remembers fields of beans that nor-
mally produced thirty bushels an acre producing only
five. "Little bitty, dried-up, shriveled beans. A year of
your life is invested in that crop and it comes time to
reap what you have sown and you don't even get back
what you've put into it."

After the harvest, Rick told Billy that he wanted to sell
out. He chanted the litany: Billy's health wasn't good,
the economy was out of control, the demand and prices
for crops were too low, the debts were increasing, the
structure of farming had changed, and the future did not
look good.

But Billy would not quit and Rick would not leave his
father with half the debt, so they kept going. To make
ends meet, Rick took a second job, a night shift factory
job, making $8.50 an hour. Not much, but better than
farming.

Right before spring planting, Billy had triple-bypass
surgery and a heart valve replaced. Pappy John was no
longer able to drive a tractor, so he ran errands in the old
truck.

Rick worked at the planting all day and then worked
all night at the factory making car axles. His mother
Sarah helped him in the fields and the neighbors helped
to get the crops planted. The corn, beans, and milo all
looked good.

In May, Billy died of a heart attack. In July, Pat told
Rick she wanted a divorce. Rick looked at the $200,000
debt and knew that it was over.

Rick still will tell you, "Farming is the best place a
person can be and the best job that a person can have if
you could only make a living at it.

"When a person does nothing but farm all day, he

works all day, and except for those times when he is pushed, he can get in at a decent hour to clean up and be with his family. And when he's got his family to look forward to coming home to, that's a hope and joy that is constant.

"It can even be an art form in that a man can get up every day and go down to the farm, get on his equipment and take pride in what he does with his hands. He can take pride in seeing how straight a row he can plant, how good a condition he can keep his field in, how clean he can keep his crops. It is a good life, the best life.

"But the farm can be the worst place you can be when you can't make a living at it. When a man's got to work the farm plus work another job, it can be h-e-double-l. Farming was the thing that turned my life around and got my head on straight. And now it has become the thing that has almost ruined my life."

One day, after hearing just such comments from Rick, Pappy John and I watched as Rick climbed onto the combine and rode in the cool November air. The old man propped himself against the tailgate of a pickup truck, thinking about the days when he used to farm sweet potatoes during the Depression, covering plants by hand, loading the harvest onto mule wagons, taking them to town for fifteen cents a bushel.

"Back in those days we had plenty to eat. We made almost everything ourselves. We bought sugar, coffee, and a can of kerosene, maybe a yard of domestic [cloth] from time to time. Grew our own wheat, took it to mill."

"Better off then?" I asked.

"I wouldn't be surprised if we weren't in a way." Pappy watches another driver relieve Rick on the combine. "I don't know much about the financial situation. I never borrowed money with Billy and Rick. But ain't no doubt in my mind that Billy worried himself into the grave."

* * *

It is 1985, the Saturday after Thanksgiving.

Rick has sold his house. The corn crop is in and has been sold, the last harvest for Rick and Sarah. Sarah and her late husband Billy's farm is about to be sold, along with all the farming equipment.

"Billy only had $30,000 insurance on this loan, and when he died, the creditors got that," says Sarah. "They got the wheat money. They got the money for the milo and the corn. They got the money from the farm we sold, and they'll get the money from the crops that are still on it as soon as they're harvested and we get paid. And the money from Rick's house, too."

All of the money has gone to pay the creditors. But it is only half of what they owe. "The one thing I hope I live to see," says Sarah, "is the debt paid off." It is not what she once hoped that she would live to see.

The sound of tractors and a combine filter into the house. It is not the sound of farmers at work; it is the sound of auctioneers heating up the engines so they will start the first time when the prospective buyers arrive.

By nine-thirty, country music is blaring from the auctioneer's camper and the crowd, mostly farmers, has begun to gather up in the yard. Rain has made the fields too wet for working, so the crowd should be good. Some inspect equipment, but most just mill around and visit with their neighbors.

"Everything Billy Capps had he took good care of."

"Ain't no fun to go to an estate sale—especially if you know the folks."

"I may be wrong—I hope I am—but I don't think it'll bring much this time of year. I'm afraid they're gonna take a beating."

"This isn't folks who went crazy with 3,000 acres or something, these are just home folks trying to make a living."

Billy's daughter Brenda looks around. "It's like a remnant of my Daddy evaporating."

The auctioneer reminds everyone to pay for all purchases before they leave the sale to do any Christmas shopping. Then he begins with the items piled up on the trailer.

A small vise goes for five dollars. One of the auctioneer's employees yawns. They have had a farm sale every Saturday in November and more are lined up. A jigsaw sells for five dollars and the auctioneer beats on the side of the camper with a stick. "If we are going to give it away, we're going to give it away fast." For some reason a Chevrolet truck hood ornament goes for thirteen dollars.

Sarah watches the proceedings from under a tree. After a while, she goes inside. Brenda tells me that Pappy John goes to the hospital tomorrow to begin chemotherapy. I hadn't heard.

The 1966 Ford truck with 45,605 miles, proclaims the auctioneer, "will do everything one of those $10,000 ones will." It sells for $4,000.

The Harvester truck, however, only brings $2,000. Folks are scared that parts will be hard to come by now

that Harvester has gone under. They get a good price for
a planter, but the grain bins go for $20,000 less than what
the Capps paid for them. The tractors are sold for prices
that turn out to be not as low as the Capps had feared.
An auctioneer's assistant brings the vehicle titles for
Rick and Sarah to sign over to the new owners.

The land is next, and it is all that there is left. "This is
what I am dreading," says Sarah quietly.

On the first tract of forty-nine acres, the auctioneer
tries to start the bidding at $50,000, then $25,000, then
lower. Sarah sits under a tree with a stick in her hand,
wearing Billy's old Illinois Central and Gulf Railroad
jacket with the American flag on the sleeve. Someone
bids $23,000. Sarah breaks the stick.

She listens for a minute or two as the bidding begins
on the next tract and then heads for the house.
Incredibly the radio is playing, "Dust in the wind, all we
are is dust in the wind."

"Did you sell the land?" Brenda asks her mother.

"It's not bringing what I had hoped, but I'm afraid
not to take it," Sarah tells her, looking away. To herself,
she says, "Get it paid. Free of worry."

She signs the papers that signify that she accepts the
bids.

The sale is over.

* * *

Billy has been gone for a decade and a half now.

A few months after the last harvest, Pappy John lost
his last fight with cancer and passed away.

Brenda and her family moved to Nashville, then to a
smaller city. They used to come down the farm road

from time to time, especially at holidays to see Sarah.

Sarah nearly lost the house again after paying off the debts and the taxes from the sale. But she was able to save it. She lived there alone for a while. Finally, she moved in with Brenda and her family.

Rick's children are grown now. If the family still had the farm, you might look across the fields and see one of them driving a combine. Instead, like Rick, they moved to another state.

With each passing day, there are fewer and fewer family farms and farmers. When their ties to the land are cut, people are set adrift, without their ground, without their grounding.

SEVEN

The Parable
of the Good Republican

I once attended a conference on what it means to be a Democrat. My attendance may have been unnecessary, for I don't know how to be anything else.

My grandparents almost lost their farm during the Depression when they could not get enough money for their crops to pay the taxes. Thanks to a judge who was a Democrat, my father had a job as a clerk in the court house and a salary to go with it. So Dad was able to pay his parents' tax bills until President Franklin Roosevelt's New Deal gave farmers a prayer—and some decent prices for their crops—again.

My Dad, so I have been told, was the youngest delegate to the 1936 Democratic National Convention. He supported, of course, President Roosevelt.

My grandfather and my great uncle Dean each served as members of the Weakley County Court for more than thirty years. Uncle Dean also was a state representative and then a senator in the forties and fifties. A couple of other relatives were sheriffs. All these were Democrats.

When my older brother Dean wanted to get married, he had to bring his prospective bride home to Weakley County to meet Mammy Grooms, the family matriarch. "Lean over here, child," the ancient woman said from her bed to the bride-to-be. Diane leaned so the lamp's light lit her face.

Mammy feebly touched her cheek gently with her gnarled old fingers. "I have but one question," she whispered. "Are you a Democrat or a Republican?"

My fully-briefed and well-prepared future sister-in-law quickly replied, "A *Democrat*, ma'am."

Mammy patted Diane's cheek. "Then you have my blessing."

In 1967, my father had a heart attack. Through the efforts of a Democrat who was Speaker of the House, a Democratic Governor appointed Dad to fill a judgeship. The lessened stress of being a judge let Dad live and serve for another nine years. When the time came for Dad to run for the judgeship, he ran, of course, as a Democrat.

Some of my earliest memories are of going with Dad to Democratic political events. I'll never forget the night Dad introduced me to our Democratic Congressman, the Honorable "Fats" Everett. When I was a high school senior, Dad arranged with Congressman Everett's successor, Congressman Ed Jones, another Democrat, for me to page two months for the U.S. House of Representatives in Washington.

To say that I was raised a good Democrat is something of an understatement.

* * *

At nineteen, my sister Betsye, a bright and beautiful young woman, married. The Homecoming Queen married the next town's football star, who would soon be flying in Air Force jets while she finished college. Betsye hung in there as long as she could, but before long they divorced and went their separate ways.

She finished college, started teaching, and met another fellow. He was the son of a lawyer, from a good family of devout Democrats, and soon they married. They blessed with a handsome son. Then came Betsye's second divorce.

Two unhappy marriages and two painful divorces pretty much stripped my sister of self-esteem and confidence. Her once-bright future had become an all too painful present.

One weekend I came home from law school and Mother told me that Betsye wanted us to come to her house for dinner. She had someone that she wanted us to meet. I was decidedly unenthusiastic at the prospect, but concluded that it was best to humor my mother and sister and also check out whatever rascal was coming around now. The clincher was that my alternative entertainment for the evening was studying for an exam in law school's most boring course, civil procedure.

* * *

I drove Mother to Betsye's home in Trenton, the next county seat south. As we drove, I asked Mother about the fellow we were to meet.

He was a doctor—that was good.

But he had been a delegate to a Republican National Convention—that sounded bad.

His father was a Baptist preacher—that could be good or bad, it was hard to tell.

He liked to cook and he was going to cook supper for us. That also could go either way, but at least I could make a clear call on that after the meal was over.

At my sister's, when the doorbell rang, Mother suggested I answer it. "You must be Roy," an old-looking fellow said. "I'm Charlie Hickman." He was obviously much too old for my sister. Closer, I thought, to my Mother's age.

As he shook my hand, however, I discovered that the old geezer had a very good grip. I tried not to show the pain as I pulled my hand away. "Don't you go to Vanderbilt Law School?" he immediately asked.

"I do," I acknowledged.

"Isn't that where that [string of expletives deleted] Albert Gore teaches?"

"No, sir," I stammered, more than a bit taken aback both by the preacher's son's language and the ferocity of his venom.

"I don't mean that no-count young one, I mean the old man. Doesn't that [expletive deleted] teach there?"

"No, sir."

My mother had warned me not to talk about politics. But apparently nobody warned Charlie. Soon, he was telling me about the glory days as a Goldwater delegate to the Republican National Convention in 1964. My sister listened like he was talking good sense. I tried not to respond. Fortunately, I suppose, he talked non-stop so much that responding wasn't an option.

So much for politics.

While Betsye went to check on something in the kitchen, Charlie and Mother and I sat down to visit in the living room. Charlie launched into telling jokes and I launched into trying to laugh. Until he told what could only charitably be called an ethnic joke. As it started, I looked down at the floor and hoped he was not headed where I suspected. When he finished, I excused myself and left the room without looking up. Mother had gotten me into this—she could deal with him.

Mother eventually stared and glared me out of the den chair to which I'd retreated. I reluctantly wandered into the kitchen as Betsye and Charlie fixed supper. Charlie wanted to talk about sports. Good, I thought, I can do that. It turned out, however, that he was an Ole Miss football fan and they had beaten my beloved Tennessee Volunteers that year. It didn't happen often, so he rubbed it in real good. He had taken my sister to the game. She had the audacity to tell me how much she had enjoyed it. Already he was making my sister forget her raising and turn against her own flesh. So much for sports.

To make things worse, he smoked like a chimney. And Betsye joined him. My contact lenses went nuts and my eyes were burning something terrible. Burning, in fact, pretty much describes how all of me was feeling. I realized that I had found perhaps the only way on earth to spend an evening that was less enjoyable than studying for a civil procedure exam.

By dinner, I was saying nothing. I was looking for the door, pretty sure that he had offended me and disagreed with me in every way possible. Of course, I was wrong.

Over the steaks, he wanted to talk about religion. He

began by inquiring about my attending divinity school. I cautiously admitted that I had. He proceeded to tell me about the great Hal Lindsey and his book, *The Late, Great Planet Earth*. The fact that I had already read it meant nothing to Charlie, who, it was clear, knew everything. He was convinced that Lindsey was right, that the world was about to end, and that it would be during our lifetime. If Lindsey is right, I thought, could the end come soon—like before Charlie opens his mouth again?

Betsye, of course, listened attentively to his every word—and there sure were a lot of them. I wanted to shake her.

* * *

Though the world did not end then, eventually the evening did. After he crunched my hand again, Mom and I started home. We were almost out of Betsye's driveway when Mother asked, "Well, what did you think of Charlie?"

I held back from saying that except for his politics, religion, racism, humor, devotion to Ole Miss, smoking, cursing and being too old for my sister, he seemed okay. Dutiful son that I am, I went for not telling the truth without telling a lie. "Well, Mom, he seems real *interesting*. What do *you* think of him?"

Mother said she thought he was real nice. I think my own mother lied to me.

* * *

A little over a month later, Charlie's eighty-something-year-old Baptist preacher father and I performed the ceremony. I was sure that Betsye was marrying too soon. Especially since she was marrying the wrong man. I took it as a divine confirmation that it wasn't right when she held out the wrong hand for the wedding ring.

To this day, I can hardly believe how that Republican rascal acted after they got married. For one thing, Betsye did not fix dinner at their house again for years. Charlie himself fixed every dinner. He would get home from work and cook for her and wait on her and insist that he enjoyed it. I think he did enjoy it, too. I know for a fact that Betsye did.

Then they carefully planned and he built her a new home, their dream home, the place she'd always wanted, on a pretty hill under huge oak trees. He took her to New Orleans to his favorite restaurants and anywhere else she wanted to go. He courted her like they were still kids and on each date he was trying to get her to go out with him again. He loved her every single way he knew how.

And my sister, whose confidence and self-esteem had almost evaporated, came back. Charlie treated her like the lovely, laughing, loving, living person that he knew she could be. And she became that person again.

But more than that. Charlie took Betsye's eight-year-old son Will and made him his very own. Charlie fixed Will a desk and a bookshelf in his room. He colored pictures and painted with him. They made model airplanes and ships. He helped him with his math problems. He saw that Will wanted for nothing. He did everything he knew to earn the boy's respect and to gain his love. He did everything anyone could do for that boy. And then he did some more.

He bought him a car when the time came, even before the time came. He took that little boy to cities and ballgames (admittedly, mostly to Ole Miss ballgames).

He raised him as his own and that little boy grew up to be as kind and compassionate a man as I know anywhere.

It was as though Dr. Charlie had found an injured woman and a wounded little boy by the side of the road and had simply taken care of them. The wounded were healed. The hurting were made whole.

I, good Democrat that I am, am still blown away by the whole thing.

Who would have thought that a Republican, and especially this particular Republican, would turn out to be The Good Samaritan?

EIGHT

Our   Prayers

*A*s long as I can remember, every night my parents said The Lord's Prayer with me. Whether they put me in my own bed or let me in theirs, when the lights were out we would talk until the sleepiest would suggest, "Let's say our prayers." And we would repeat together: "Our Father who art in heaven, hallowed be thy name . . . ."

I never prayed on my knees like the children in the paintings. Usually we prayed as I lay in bed between Mother and Dad, before they would take me to my bed, or Mother would give up and go to it herself. Sometimes Mother would come into my brother Ben's and my bedroom and she alone would say our prayers with us. Often we would go back to the bedroom where Dad already was asleep. Ben or I would shake his big arm with a tiny hand, "Daddy, Daddy, wake up and let's say our prayers." Then we would pray The Lord's Prayer together. Sometimes before we would finish, Dad would fall back asleep, leaving us to conclude together.

We also prayed together before meals. I don't recall us ever eating at home without saying what Dad called "Grace" or Mother called "The Blessing." Mother and Dad, having been through the Depression, always were thankful. And they knew Whom to thank.

Despite our daily rituals, I never thought of my parents as particularly religious. We never had Bible study together, unlike the Bennett family whose daughters were in school and church with us. I don't recall my father owning a Bible other than a big one he inherited, nor did I see him read it. Though a lifelong Cumberland Presbyterian, Dad always came with us to Sunday School at the United Methodist Church, Mother's church. But after Sunday School sometimes he would slip out and walk home. Mother explained that the wooden pews hurt Dad when he had to sit still for so long.

* * *

On Sunday nights, when Mother and Dad often went out to eat, they would leave Ben and me with Miss Garthelia Lewis. Our parents would take us by her house, a block from the courthouse and four blocks from our house, in the part of town polite whites called Colored Town.

Miss Garthelia's house had a softdrink machine, which made her one of the town's few black business-people, her and the bootleggers. After we'd had a soft drink, she would take my brother and me a hundred feet down the street to the Fuller Street Baptist Church. There during the Sunday night singing and preaching, clapping and shouting, praising and praying, my brother and I would stretch out on the back pew, our feet pointing in opposite directions, our heads often touching and always resting on Miss Garthelia's church-going dress in the softest lap. She had the gentlest touch as she stroked our hair and touched our faces with her fingertips as we fell asleep. I still don't know how she got us back to her house, for we would awaken, if then, only when Mother and Dad came by her home to take us to ours.

* * *

When I was about seven, I encountered and wrestled with the Unknown. I was at home, wandering down the hallway with its dark wooden floor. It was a Sunday evening and something said at church that morning was bothering me.

I was wondering who made God. Who created the Creator? What was before God? How did God get here? I asked Mother and Dad, who made God? Each said God had been from the beginning.

But how can that be? Something had to make God, didn't It?

The chills, the fear went through me. And when I am not too caught up playing God myself, they linger still. And I know that this is all impossible. Impossible from our perspective. When I am quiet, I still can feel the fear and awe I felt then, realizing there's no explaining it; there's no way this makes sense.

* * *

The First United Methodist Church building in Dresden, Tennessee is a large brick structure. A building worthy of a county seat church, it is located a block south and east of the courthouse, on a higher hill. I always knew that in our church building God dwelt in the sanctuary, the sacred sanctuary.

When I was growing up, the three pairs of big wooden front doors at the front were always unlocked. Always. Sometimes I would run up the concrete steps, tug a big door open, then slowly slip into the foyer. If no one was inside, I would quietly enter the sanctuary itself. I walked softly, for God was there, and I did not want to disturb the Almighty.

The stained glass windows on the north and south sides were huge, the largest I'd ever seen, the largest in our town or anywhere around, and more beautiful than any. The light came softly through them, illuminating Jesus' face and hands. And there Jesus stood six times, in three windows on each side, with a Gospel verse below each painting of our Lord.

I would slip down one of the two aisles and take a seat on an old wooden pew, dark and hard as oak, which it was. I would stare at the illuminated cross hanging behind the choir seats, in front of the huge, golden metal pipes that made the organ so special on Sunday mornings.

The sanctuary, even on a sunny day, would be dark, and quieter still because of the darkness and shadows. The sanctuary had the highest ceiling I'd ever seen. And the entire room was simple, uncluttered. The colors were solid and strong: off-white walls and ceiling, dark brown

wooden pews and pulpit and choir loft and chancel railing, purple kneeling cushions, the golden organ pipes,
the white lights.

There was the sense of the sacred, that God was here
or at least watched while I was there, and cared about
how I treated His house, His room, His special place.

And yet, it was a comfortable place. A place of securi-
ty. Of comfort from whatever ailed me, whenever something troubled me.

* * *

In Sunday School we sang again and again:

Jesus loves the little children,
all the children of the world.
Red and yellow, black and white,
they are precious in His sight.
Jesus loves the little children of the world.

But even as our mothers taught us this song, our
fathers made sure that men guarded the church and pro-
tected us from those who were different from us. "Why
are they there?" we asked. Mother explained that some
black people might be trying to come into our church
and cause trouble. So the men were outside to make sure
there was no trouble.

The black people never came that Sunday. Not even a
single black would come for several years. Black children might be precious in Jesus' sight, but their parents
were something else, at least if they wanted in our sanctuary. Except, of course, to clean it.

* * *

We also learned "Jesus Loves the Little Children" in Vacation Bible School. And not just at the Methodist church, either. For most of the year the denominations grumbled about each other, but each summer the mothers found unity on one issue: their kids could go to all the Vacation Bible Schools. Denominationalism and pew prejudice were set aside in the cause of getting youngsters out of their mothers' hair for a few hours as many mornings as possible.

I will never forget one Vacation Bible School at the Church of Christ building. I was tiny, probably preschool still. I asked the teacher where the bathroom was. She told me to go through one door and another one and I would find the bathroom.

So, I went out and went through one door, then through another. There were steps past this second door, but I did not hesitate. I quickly started down the steps and in an instant I was in water up to my neck.

The water was warm, greenish blue, and very pretty. I decided to swim a bit. I swam to the far side and back, much of the swim under water where the colors and the light shining on the bottom made it all the prettier. Finally, no longer feeling a need to go to the bathroom, I got out. It is recalled that when I walked back to the classroom, water still dripping off me, I told the teacher, "If I'd known you had a swimming pool, I'd have come here before."

Some of my friends in the Dresden Church of Christ feel this sprinkled Methodist's best hope of eternal salvation occurred with my immersion that summer morning. They may be right. I'm not arguing with anyone pulling for me.

* * *

The most memorable preaching I ever heard occurred not in a church building, but in the open air on the Court Square.

Charlie Bruce seemed quite old when I first saw him—and heard him. He would appear regularly at the court square, back when people would "come to town" on Saturdays, back before national chains ran local merchants out of business, when the court square instead of the Wal-Mart was the center of commerce.

Charlie Bruce would come to the court square and place himself on the courthouse lawn on the east, west, or south sides—and he moved so fast he appeared to be on all three at once. The lawn on those three sides was higher than the street, so Charlie was elevated above those who parked around the square. Like a hawk for Jesus, he would swoop down upon persons parking their cars and trucks. Most people would scramble quickly to get away, running into one store or another. Anyone innocent or foolish enough to try to sit in a vehicle did not last long. Brother Charlie Bruce would come at his prey, yelling so loudly that we could hear him on the opposite side of the square. Yelling so loudly that he covered his own ears with his hands.

"Jesus is coming soon! Jesus is coming soon! I mean soon, very soon, brother! Many will not be ready! Will you be ready? Or will you be plunged into the lake of eternal hellfire and damnation? Will you be plunged into that pit of pain? Better get ready! Better get ready! Get ready!"

And he would go on and on and on. All day on Saturday. All day no matter how hot, no matter how

sweat-soaked his white shirt or the white handkerchief
he whipped out and swiped over his bald head and
sweaty cheeks. All day until no more sinners came
downtown. Yelling and proclaiming the bad news—
which I guess might have become good news if people
had listened to him and changed their ways. Maybe
someone did.

* * *

Most of the preaching I heard growing up was not so
loud, so plaintive, so intense. Our Methodist preachers
were almost always gentle men. Not one preached like
Brother Charlie Bruce, at least not when I was at church.
When I was young, Methodist preachers moved often,
still riding the circuit in a manner. So we had several
while I was growing up, but some stand out even now.

The Reverend Jerry Hassell must have come along
when I was in junior high school. I would sit in the balcony while Brother Hassell preached. He made me want
to listen at a time when I didn't listen much to anyone.
He taught me when I thought I already knew almost
everything worth knowing. He would close his sermons
with an invitation to make a decision, a decision that he
and God wanted me to make. He would tell me somehow—maybe not explicitly, but clearly—that I could do
better, I could be better, God would help me. Sunday
after Sunday I was filled with emotion, wanted to be better, committed to do differently.

Brother Hassell taught our confirmation class. He
took us through the Apostles' Creed, line by line and
phrase by phrase. He was honest with us when we
asked hard questions, even when his honesty was not

ultra-orthodox and scared some of us—and intrigued others. I must have been sick or out of town the Sunday I was supposed to be confirmed, so I had to wait a year and be confirmed with the kids a year younger. But it was no big deal. Or at least not as big a deal as it might ought to have been. In any event, Brother Hassell got me through it.

* * *

I cannot recall much about Sunday School classes. A friend says this is because it was not so much the lessons taught as the lessons lived, not so much the words but the relationships. And, he pointed out, it was not a single teacher, but rather a team effort collectively loving us.

The women of our church were God's women. They were our other mothers and aunts and grandmothers, our neighbors and friends, each with her history and connectedness to my parents, grandparents and siblings. My grandmother, Miss Johnnie, had taught not a few of my teachers. These women cared about me before I was born, nurtured me in the nursery, taught me the hymns for Christmas plays, bragged on me when I was growing up, expected good from me even when I was not, loved me always. Never once, not for a second, have I doubted that they loved my family and they loved me. When ministers preached about God's unconditional love, I understood. These church women had shown me what all-accepting love was, is, and ever shall be.

* * *

The church men I never confused with saints. A few seemed so upright, so proper, so dignified that I imagined they could have been Biblical prophets. That was before I learned prophets were rowdy types—and these men were anything but rowdy.

Most of the church men, however, had plenty of little boy left in them. They teased us, joked with us, played with us. If the church women were the embracing arms and tender voices, the church men were laughing eyes and big smiles.

Some were Dad's fellow attorneys. Others were merchants, with the small town merchants' charm. Some were grocers, who sold us pints of chocolate milk or fixed us baloney sandwiches even when we ran a few cents or nickels short. Others were farmers who hired me to haul hay or doctors who treated me when I was sick, or fitted me for glasses.

Outside the church, I knew them by their professions. But at the church I knew them as the men who taught Sunday School, sang in the choir, or sat and stood in the same spot each Sunday. I knew the ushers who stayed outside on pretty spring mornings talking to us until they had to go in and collect the offering. Sometimes they would be a man or two short of the needed six and would enlist a boy or two to walk solemnly down the two aisles with them before we were prayed over and passed the plates. Then the choir led the congregation in one song whose words we all knew:

Praise God, from whom all blessings flow;
Praise him all creatures here below;
Praise him above, ye heavenly host;
Praise Father, Son, and Holy Ghost.
Amen.

Like the women, the men of the church were there.
Sunday after Sunday. Most were there every Sunday,
regardless of the weather, hunting, fishing, golf, or anything else. By their presence, they taught that church
was important, and that I needed to pay attention to
God. I tried to remember when I went to college, eight
miles up the road at the University of Tennessee campus
in my home county.

* * *

It was a pretty September afternoon, but I was inside
a dorm. I was running for freshman class representative,
so I was knocking on doors. I rapped on one door next
to the eye-level "Jesus Saves" sticker and listened to the
guitar music coming from inside.

The door opened and standing there were two guys
with what in 1971 was not a lot of hair, but more than I
had. Two guys with crosses around their necks, one
wooden and anything but discreet and the other made
of enough metal to cause neck strain. Two guys grinning
like they were awfully pleased to see me.

"Hey, brother, I'm Barry!" one guy said so happily
you'd have thought he was on something.

"And I'm Steve," the other one smiled, extending his
hand forward, too.

"I'm Roy," I replied, adding as I nodded toward their
door, "I like your sticker." That was all the opening they
needed. They went after me like I was a can and they
were can openers.

"Are you a Christian, brother?" Barry asked.

"Yes."

"If you died right now," Steve asked, "would you go
to heaven?"

"Well, I guess that's for God to say, but I'd hope so."

"Oh, brother, don't you *know*?"

If I hadn't been campaigning, I'd have turned heel and fled.

They cross-examined me relentlessly. They asked if I knew about The Four Spiritual Laws—I didn't. If I knew Jesus as my Personal Savior—I thought I did. If I was in a campus Bible study—I wasn't, but I'd like to be. If I wanted to grow in the Lord—sure, I said, but thought to myself, What's the alternative: shrinking out of the Lord?

I had never met anyone my own age so intense, so fired up and determined to save the world, or at least its inhabitants. I finally extracted myself by repeatedly promising to attend a "Live Now" program a few nights later.

Steve and Barry had said they would be there. I went anyway. When I did not see them in the crowd of a couple of hundred students in the University Center ballroom, I sat near the back, so I could slip out early and easy.

The speaker didn't talk about the devil and hell-fire, like Charlie Bruce, or about Jesus and love, like my pastors. Instead, he talked about the Holy Spirit. He talked about God dwelling within us. He talked about following the Spirit. He talked about the Holy Spirit taking control of our lives.

And he talked about "selling out to the Lord." He told stories of people who had been totally committed to the Lord. Some of them were Bible characters—like the Apostle Paul. He asked if we were willing to commit all of our lives to the Lord. Now he was stepping on my toes, for parts of my life I didn't want God even to know about, much less take my shortcomings or pleasures away. He asked, "Do you want to give God control of every part of your life?" The answer to that question was not "No" but "Heavens no."

I thought I was more committed than some other guys. But the idea of making God the Lord of every part of my life was at best unappealing and at worst terribly frightening.

The music started up again and the evangelist had us all bow our heads. "With every head bowed and every eye closed, I want you to be honest with God. I want you to be honest with God, especially if you are afraid to be honest with yourself. Are you one hundred percent committed to God? If you're not, raise your hand."

I raised my hand.

He told us to think about those areas of our lives that we did not want to turn over to God. To think about the pain we were causing others, the pain we might be causing ourselves. To think about how God wants all of us, not just part of us.

"If you want God to change your life, to take your life, to take control of your life, raise your hand."

I hesitated, but eventually again raised my hand.

Then the evangelist hit the altar call button. And I struggled to stay in my seat. "If you want God to change your life, now is the time. This is the place. Come down to the front and let God take your burdens, let the Spirit touch you and make you who God wants you to be."

I knew he was right: I was tired of trying to control my own life, tired of messing things up, tired of holding back from God. Why shouldn't I turn my life over to God? Wasn't that what I ought to do?

Finally, I went down front. Soon Barry and Steve were there with me, putting their hands on my shoulders, praying for me. And I asked God to "become the Lord of my life. Take my life, take *all* of my life." And through tears of sadness at all of my shortcomings and failures and sins came tears of joy.

Before or since, with the possible exception of the births of our children, I have never felt such joy and peace.

* * *

In the months afterward, one day at a time I tried to honor that commitment to God. Steve and Barry and others reminded me that I had to get my roots deeper in God's Word and had to find faithful fellowship if I was to keep my commitment and if I was to grow. "There's no standing still," they reminded me, "for you'll either grow closer to God or shirk away from God, but you won't stand still."

Seeking to grow, I went to the Baptist Student Union (BSU) and found friendly but fiercely committed people. The BSU director was a young, open guy we called "Rabbi" who encouraged me. My own Methodist student center was a couple of buildings north of the BSU. There the minister told a group of us we ought to consider the ordained ministry. I laughed at him. At first.

The chancellor at our campus was in his thirties, with three degrees from Yale, including one that made him a Disciples of Christ minister. As I got to know Larry and his wife Betsy, I began to think one might be a minister without being imprisoned in a pulpit. I was not ready to give up my plans for law school, but I did want to study the Bible more—I was running into too many questions and needed some answers.

In the meantime, I was hanging out with friends, playing student politics both on campus and beyond. One year I was elected to an office in a state organization of college students. Two close classmates who also had attained offices had come back to Dresden to spend the night. I awoke early, still happy about our successes of the day before, but suddenly worried because it was Sunday morning and one of my guests was black.

I went back to Mother and Dad's bedroom. I told them of our victories and that Mike and Emmett had come home with me. I told them there was, however, one problem. If Emmett were not with us, I said, this morning Mike and I would go to church. And if Emmett were white, we would go to church. But I did not recall a black person attending our church. So, what did they think?

Dad did not hesitate. "You go ahead and do what you think is right." And he turned back to his newspaper. I looked at Mother. She grinned and told me she had better start fixing breakfast, or else we would be late for church.

I awoke Mike and Emmett with the good news and the bad news: Mother was fixing breakfast, but she wouldn't bring it to them in bed. Besides, if they didn't get up, they'd be late for church. That brought a groan from Mike, but Emmett sat straight up, fully awake, and said church would not be necessary. I told him his bed-mate needed to attend and I had already talked with Dad.

After breakfast, the three of us walked the block to

church. We got there late, which suited us fine. I took a church bulletin from a startled usher, and we slipped up to the balcony. The congregation was standing, singing a hymn. As we sang, I noticed Reverend Hassell turning to look behind him in the choir loft, and I saw one choir member had stopped singing, a man who had promised the pastor that he would walk out if an African-American ever attended our service. But the service went right on and no one left.

After the benediction, we fled down the stairs, but not quickly enough. "Roy," one of the gray-haired ladies said as she blocked our exit and stuck her hand out to Emmett, "introduce me to your friend." Ignoring Mike, she told Emmett, "We are so glad you joined us for worship and we sure hope Roy will bring you back!" Other worshippers clustered around, eager to welcome Emmett. Most ignored the six-foot-three Mike—probably the first time in his life he'd been overlooked.

Others passed by and smiled. Just as I began to relax, a retired gentleman who had long been special to me walked past, stopping only long enough to scowl, first at Emmett, then at me. I'd never seen his face so cold or angry, and because he'd been one of my teachers and was a dear friend, I ached. But he was the only one. To my surprise and Emmett's relief, Emmett had to shake more hands than the preacher.

On the walk home, Mike and I laughed and even Emmett smiled with relief. I was joyful that those who had taught me about Jesus loving all the children had loved Emmett, too.

Mother Love

My mother was born in 1916 in the "Sweet Potato Capital of the World," Gleason, Tennessee. A few months later, her parents moved eight miles to Dresden, to a house two blocks from the Court Square and two blocks from the city limits. On that same small lot, Mother has lived seven of her eight decades, and she lives there still.

* * *

When Mother was a tiny baby, John Irvine, the proprietor of Irvine's Grocery, would call my grandmother on sunny days and tell her, "Johnnie, get the baby ready; I'm going to take her around today and show her off."

Mr. Irvine would bring Miss Johnnie's groceries and empty the wire basket on her kitchen table. Then they would place a pillow in the basket, gently lay Mother on it, and cover her with a baby blanket. Mr. Irvine would leave with Mother swinging in the basket on his arm. He would place her carefully next to him on the seat and slowly drive his horse and wagon around town. Each time he made a delivery, he would carry the basket with Mother in one hand and a basket of groceries in the other. They would go to the back door, where the delighted customer always insisted they come in so she could coo over the new baby, Mary Cornelia Brasfield.

Maybe John Irvine was just shrewd at marketing. But as Mother grew up hearing this story, she always felt special. And she was.

* * *

When we were children, Mother often told my younger brother Ben and me about ancient ancestors. She reminded us our people fought for the Colonies in the Revolutionary War. She claimed that in the Battle of King's Mountain no less than nine relatives, a father and eight sons, were killed. But her favorite story was about an ancestor named Reuben Edmonston.

"Now, your several-greats-grandfather, Reuben Edmonston, was the first settler here in Weakley County," Mother would brag. "He and his brother-in-law John Bradshaw came here in 1819, when no one was around except the Chickasaw Indians. They built the first log cabin in the county and raised the first patch of corn. They settled on Mud Creek, about six miles from here towards Martin—but of course there was no Dresden or Martin back then. There wasn't even a Weakley County until four years later.

"You've heard about Davy Crockett," Mother would say, knowing we'd seen the movie and devotedly watched the television show. "People think Davy Crockett was such a great frontiersman, but he *followed* your ancestor Reuben Edmonston to West Tennessee. Davy Crockett owned land in Weakley County, too, not far from our farm at the Forks of the River.

"You know Davy Crockett was the champion bear hunter. But do you know who was second? Your ancestor Reuben Edmonston. One year Davy killed over 100 bears, but Reuben got almost as many—eighty-nine, I think."

I wondered why she told these old tales of ancient ancestors. Then one day I realized she wished she'd been a pioneer.

* * *

To understand Mother, and why she'd have liked being a pioneer, you have to understand her parents.

Mother's father, Roy Brasfield, became a pharmacist in 1913. Some said the center of activity in Dresden was the Alexander & Brasfield drug store. If so, the epicenter was the drug store's soda fountain, where Mother was allowed all of the ice cream, sundaes, and milkshakes she wanted, though most fountain drinks and all candies were forbidden her.

Mr. Roy proved himself a popular friend and a successful businessman. He needed to succeed, because many customers could pay little or nothing. He filled their prescriptions just the same, as long as they tried to pay something, or if they were unable to work. He also needed to make a profit because his wife, Miss Johnnie, was becoming the town's unpaid social worker.

When Miss Johnnie moved to Dresden, she had immediately joined the First Methodist Episcopal Church. She thought the church doors could not open without her entering: Sunday mornings, Sunday evenings, Wednesday Bible study. Her Missionary Society met on Mondays—and their work continued through the week. It seemed to Mother that if the sun came up, Miss Johnnie went down to the church.

Miss Johnnie took Mister Jesus mighty seriously. She read and re-read those troubling words about The Great Judgment. She could quote the 25th chapter of Matthew from memory and often did, teaching her daughter and reminding her neighbors:

> For I was an hungred, and ye gave me meat; I was thirsty, and ye gave me drink; I was a stranger, and ye took me in;
>
> Naked, and ye clothed me; I was sick, and ye visited me; I was in prison, and ye came unto me.
>
> Then shall the righteous answer him, saying, Lord, when saw we thee an hungred, and fed thee? or thirsty, and gave thee drink?
>
> When saw we thee a stranger, and took thee in? or naked, and clothed thee?
>
> Or when saw we thee sick, or in prison, and came unto thee?
>
> And the King shall answer and say unto them, Verily I say unto you, Inasmuch as ye have done it unto one of the least of these my brethren, ye shall have done it unto me. (King James Version.)

When Miss Johnnie died in 1952, a Memphis newspaper reported, "She was what the town said was an 'angel of mercy,' visiting in homes in Dresden whenever there was sorrow or distress, bearing messages of cheer and good will."

But Miss Johnnie went bearing more than messages. Barely five feet tall, she walked rapidly all over town, taking whatever the sick needed and the poor could not afford. Baskets of groceries for the hungry. Home-cooked meals for the sick. Clean sheets for poor women to lie on as they gave birth. Medicines from her husband's drug store, knowing that many could never pay and no one was ever billed. When the Mississippi River flooded, she spent weeks at the church, cooking and caring for the refugees, many of them poor sharecroppers. When the Depression hit, she just did more of the same.

She did what she did, like many church women and some men, because Jesus told her to. She knew what Jesus taught because she herself taught "the littlest children." Miss Johnnie went out and gathered children for her Sunday School class. She convinced parents to let their children come, even when poverty made those parents reluctant to attend the Methodist Church where the more affluent went. And for more than thirty years she gathered the children around her "horseshoe table" and showed how Jesus loved them.

Miss Johnnie has been dead almost a half-century, yet people still tell me, "Your grandmother taught me in Sunday School. She loved us so and I loved her!" Those who knew her and know my mother tell me I didn't miss a thing. They have seen her faithful compassion and love live on in my mother.

* * *

Mother's father, Mr. Roy, was less angelic. At times he was even a bit devilish, inviting preachers for a quiet drink in his kitchen, much to his teetotaling wife's chagrin. But he still gave medicines and supplies to those he knew could never pay. And he paid the bills for the sheets and groceries his wife gave the poor and sick.

While Mr. Roy sometimes complained about his wife's unconventional ways, he encouraged his daughter to do everything she could. He was determined not to let her gender or others' sexism stop or even slow his darling girl, who was never still, always getting into things, always having too much to do. By the time Mother was five, a neighbor had nicknamed her "Friskie," and that suited Mr. Roy—and Mother—just fine.

Mr. Roy taught Mother to swim so early that she never remembered when she couldn't. She swam as well or better than the boys, which created problems. When Mother was nine years old, her Sunday School Class went to Fulton, Kentucky, to a real swimming pool (instead of a river or a pond). Mother played with the girls at what she considered "the baby end" of the pool, but then decided she would swim with the boys in the deep end. Her Sunday School teacher, Dr. Jones, didn't like it, and told Mother so, but she stubbornly stayed with the boys.

Mother was sick the next Sunday so she missed Sunday School, but a cousin went and heard Dr. Jones tell about the girl who swam with the boys and how her behavior was "unladylike and unChristian." The next morning, still furious, Mr. Roy marched off to see Dr. Jones and told him he had no right to try to keep Mother "down there with the sissy girls." Furthermore, he made it clear he did not appreciate Dr. Jones talking about his beloved daughter.

That wasn't the last time Mother refused to stay in her place and her father supported her independence. When Mother wanted to rollerskate with older kids to another town, she knew better than to ask her mother. Instead, she went to Mr. Roy, who listened to her pleas and recognized her impatience at his hesitation. He pointed out the round-trip would be almost twenty miles. "I know," Mother impatiently replied. "But, please, can I, *please*, Daddy?" Mr. Roy then smiled and said, "If you think you can do it, you can." And she did.

Soon stories came back to the drug store of more skating escapades. Near his store was a hill with a sidewalk and several concrete steps. Mr. Roy was amused when customers would tell him that "your daredevil daughter" was skating down the sidewalk, jumping the steps, and landing on the sidewalk below. He was proud that only two children in town, the other an older boy, would even attempt the leap.

* * *

One year when the fair came to town, so did a barnstorming airplane that took passengers up for short rides. When Miss Johnnie heard about it, she expressly prohibited Mother from getting in that plane. So Mother went to the drug store and begged her father to take her in the plane. He responded, "You know your mother would not be amused if she found out we did such."

"Then, Daddy," my mother smiled, "we simply musn't tell her."

Soon they were at the Fairgrounds, in a crowd where everyone knew everyone else, waiting their turn to fly.

Mother sat in Mr. Roy's lap in the back of the two-seater open-cockpit biplane and they took to the air. He wasted no time in directing the pilot toward the Court Square so they could wave to the crowd. Then Mr. Roy could not resist the temptation, and he pointed the pilot toward the little house on the corner of Cedar and Main, and had him repeatedly buzz their home—and Miss Johnnie.

* * *

Mother's parents wanted her to avoid the fate of most young women at that time: no education beyond high school and an early marriage. They told her of their plans to send her to a fine women's college. But Mother, always strong-willed, had other plans. She had met a young man from Greenfield, twelve miles away. He was four years older, perhaps too much older, but handsome, well-mannered, and from a good family. And she fell hard for him.

Four decades later, I was a high school senior when I asked Mother to come help me start the car whose battery had died the night before on a country road. She asked if I'd been alone when the battery died, knowing that I had not been. As I drove us closer to the car, Mother started grinning. By the time we got within a half mile of the town's teenage parking spot, Mother started chuckling. As we pulled around a corner and the car came into view, Mother laughed out loud. My seventeen-year-old pride already plenty wounded, I told her it was not funny.

"Oh, yes, it is," she quickly replied. "This is exactly where your father and I went forty years ago."

* * *

"Everyone," Mother recalls, "was going out of state to marry. It seemed the thing to do. Very few people had any money for big weddings." On October 28, 1934, nine days after she turned eighteen, Mother and Dad eloped to Wickliffe, Kentucky. In the home of the official who sold marriage licenses, a Methodist minister married them.

They returned to their parents' homes that evening, determined to keep the secret of their wedding. Mother continued her senior year of high school. She hid her wedding ring above the transom in her bedroom, sneaking it out in her shoe and wearing it only when she and Dad were alone.

In December, Dad fell very ill. His mother grew so worried that she told him if he would just get well, she'd do anything for him. Why, he could even marry that little girl over in Dresden. Dad opened his eyes, looked straight at her, and said, "I already did."

His shocked mother fled the room to find her husband and share the awful news. Clarence, however, liked Mother and was pleased. He quickly called the drug store, told Mr. Roy the news, and suggested, "I guess this married couple ought to live together. If it's acceptable to you, Mr. Brasfield, I'll be over this afternoon to pick Mary up."

Mr. Roy was disappointed and angry; his and Miss Johnnie's plans for college the next year were suddenly moot. At noon he left the drug store and walked the two blocks home to meet Mother, who came home for lunch each day. They sat on the steps by the furnace, their special talking place. He told her, "You've played the devil, young lady, but I'll stick with you."

Meanwhile, Miss Johnnie was in the kitchen, weeping, deeply hurt because her daughter had not had a church wedding. And perhaps she wept because she had dreamed of a very different life for her daughter.

Mother and Dad lived with his parents and she commuted from Greenfield to finish high school. In a couple of years, they had my older brother, followed four years later by my sister. Then came the war.

* * *

Mother survived the war and Dad's absence with the help of her parents and friends. But after the war, life got harder.

Dad had entered a Memphis hospital again, with still more complications from his war wounds. He was fighting life-threatening infections and the doctors were recommending amputating at least one leg. Meanwhile, my brother Dean also was in a hospital, the one at Paris, Tennessee seriously ill with pneumonia. At that time, many died of pneumonia and Mother feared her first-born would be another. At the same time, my sister was at home with measles and fevers of 104 and 105. Back then measles was a killer and Betsye was in grave danger. Mother was running from hospital to home to hospital, over and over, back and forth, taking care of everyone all at once. One day, hurrying out of the hospital to go see Betsye, she fell down the stairs. Soon, she miscarried.

How did she deal with everything, with the threats to

the lives of her husband and children, with the loss of the life within her? I don't know. She says she didn't know what else to do but pray and keep on going. Unfortunately, perhaps even tougher times came later, after I was born.

* * *

When my younger brother Ben and I were growing up, Dad had sober days and lots of them. In fact, almost all the days we shared with him he was sober. Then he was the most wonderful and loving father and husband anyone could want. His nights, however, sometimes were different. He would come in from work and go to the cabinet where the bottles were. Sometimes he drank but a little. At other times, he drank too much. I can still see Mother trying to maneuver him back to the bedroom, trying to keep him from going out and driving off.

I once asked Mother about the toughest thing she ever encountered and she replied without hesitation: "Your Daddy's drinking. That was the only time he wasn't in pain. And I understood. But I hated the drinking with a passion. He was a good man, just—ooohh," and she shuddered. "I blamed myself for a long time. What have I done? What could I do? From the second drink on, he was difficult. From the fourth one he was mean . . . He never hit me but one time. And then he choked me one time.

"He followed me from the kitchen to the bedroom. He pushed me against the chest of drawers and grabbed me by the throat. You were seven or eight at the time. You tried to come in there and he told you to get away from the door. You knew something was wrong.

"He never was drunk, he thought, when he was that a way. He couldn't stand up many a time and he wasn't drunk." So Mother would try to get Ben and me out of the way, then she'd ask Dad to lie down with her, or hide the car keys, or stand in his way when he tried to go get in the car.

I do not excuse my father for the way he treated my mother. But I don't condemn him for what professionals call "self-medicating." In fact, I am in awe that he endured the pain he did, as well as he did, for as long as he did. I could not have endured his pain for three days, much less three decades. But I am at least as amazed that Mother endured both the pain Dad suffered and also the pain he inflicted.

* * *

I grew up in the same house where Mother grew up, the same house where she still lives. Within two blocks of Mother's home in her lifetime have lived the governor, a state public service commissioner, at least five mayors, five state legislators, four or five judges, a county judge and a county executive, other courthouse officials, and countless members of the county court, the county commission, and the city council.

We were two houses down and across the street from Aunt Carrie Pentecost, who long was the center of politics in Weakley County and some would maintain in Tennessee. As her son once observed: "Tom Seaver could stand in Mother's front yard and throw a baseball not more than twice, maybe just once, and hit where every one of these elected officials lived." When Aunt Carrie's kinfolks came to visit, they included our neigh-

bor and her great-nephew, Governor Ned McWherter,
her niece and nephew, Pauline Gore who was one of the
first women to graduate from Vanderbilt Law School
and Pauline's husband Senator Albert Gore, Sr., and her
great-nephew, then Senator and later Vice-President Al
Gore.

But the neighborhood was filled not only with "the e-
lite and the po-lite" of politics. In most every house were
those who might not be blood kin but who watched over
Mother and then my siblings and me like aunts and
uncles, or even mothers and fathers. And we knew they
watched over and after us. Maybe that's why Mother
only left her Cedar Street home briefly and always came
back to the same spot of ground. Because she knew how
she had been watched over and loved and she wanted
nothing less for her own children.

* * *

My wife says Mother is the epitome of her generation
of Southern womanhood. A genuine confluence of
Southern respectability and a deeply generous heart. A
college friend who spent a weekend with us went back
to the city and, referring to the character on "The Andy
Griffith Show," declared, "I just met the real Aunt Bea."
Another visitor, who later became my bride, had to learn
not to compliment Mother's antiques and decorations,
because every time she did Mother would try to give
them to her.

Mother frets over any negative remarks "being told
around town" while preening over positive comments,
especially concerning her children or grandchildren. She
was in her seventies before she would go to the drug

store without first having her hair done and without
stockings, pumps, and a matching purse.

Her uniquely Southern double name, Mary Cornelia,
usually is pronounced something like "MA-REE CA-
NEE-EEL-YA." My cousins from North Carolina
thought until they were teenagers that her name was
American Eagle.

Mother always has insisted, as her own parents did,
that every question from an elder be answered with
"Yes, Ma'am" or "No, Ma'am," "Yes, Sir" or "No, Sir."
For Mother, this is not some empty gesture or dead
litany, but a sign of respect for the hearer—and
respectability for the speaker. Recently a dear friend of
Mother's died. They had known each other for eight
decades and had helped each other through many
crises, including the almost simultaneous deaths of their
husbands. The friend was older than Mother, so until the
day the woman died Mother referred to her as Mrs.
Riggs.

Despite Mother's deep concern for both respect and
respectability, our door was open to anyone in need,
regardless of social status. Mother simply has always
been the most accepting, embracing, warmest person I
have ever known. She learned these values from her
mother, her father, and the neighbors and friends who
loved them and her.

One area family was infamous as the poorest, as well
as the most prolific. At any mention of the family, we
kids made faces and made fun. Of course, it was this
family's children Mother brought home to bathe, de-lice,
put in new clothes, brag on and love on. When she
returned them to our elementary school, she kissed the

children. The little girl hugged Mother's neck and would not let go. Mother's actions created a stir among some of our friends, but she went right ahead.

Nor did she stop after she created an even bigger stir by giving some family burial plots to a couple with lots of illness, not much life expectancy, and no money. Mother soon heard that some friends with plots nearby were upset. It wasn't fit for "those people" to be buried there, they said, and what was Mary Cornelia thinking?

"I don't know why they care," Mother sadly but defiantly told my wife. "They'll be dead then and it won't matter who they're next to."

* * *

Many times we'd come in from school to find some struggling soul at our kitchen table. "I was just going," the woman often would explain. "Just wanted to see your Mama a bit." There were women whose children or grandchildren were hurting or ill. Sometimes the children came needing a kind adult to care. Sometimes it was their mothers, struggling with husbands or without them. Those at the kitchen table included a neighbor who never seemed quite right, some great pain having bent her so. Those that others refused to listen to, Mother invited in and made feel at home. "We all need friends," she would say.

* * *

Mornings were Mother's time of day. I suppose I would think so because when I was a baby she and Dad would wake me up at three and four o'clock in the morning to play with me. When later I demanded to know why they had done such a silly thing, Mother sheepishly replied that they had not had a baby around in a long time.

When I was a little older, I returned the favor by coming back into their bed in the wee hours of the morning. She would let me snuggle between her and Dad. Many mornings Dad would get coffee for both of them and bring it back to the bedroom, and Mother would sit on the side of the bed, rubbing his painful legs. They would drink their coffee and talk and enjoy that time together. I would pretend to be asleep. They would pretend to think I was asleep, then say those things they wanted me to hear. "Aren't we proud of him?" "Isn't he just the finest boy?"

* * *

Christmas is Mother's time of year, and she never shines more brightly. None of the children or grandchildren gets more excited than Mother. The whole house has to be decorated. Every room has to have her special touches. She puts little red construction paper hats with white cotton ball trim on her father's old wooden duck decoys. The big candle, started six decades ago by dripping smaller candles onto a wine bottle, has to be placed by the door, so guests can stop and drip more wax on it. The tree ought to be a live cedar from our farm, hung with multi-colored lights that somehow, even while sitting quietly in boxes in the attic, become impossibly tangled and have to be wrestled with before they can be strung again.

When Ben and I started duck hunting together on Christmas Day, Mother still insisted we all open our gifts first thing that morning. "It wouldn't be Christmas morning if we didn't open gifts," she explained. So, to leave the house by four o'clock, Mother and Dad and Ben and I would get up at two-thirty or three to celebrate the day. While we males staggered sleepily, Mother bounced around like the labrador puppy we used to hunt with, excitedly pointing at packages, and loving on us almost more than we could stand at that hour.

* * *

Mother grew up between two of the finest fishing lakes in the South. To the east was Kentucky Lake, created by a Tennessee Valley Authority dam. To the west was Reelfoot Lake, formed by the earthquakes of 1811 and 1812. Before I was born, Mom developed into a first-class fisherwoman. She would take loads of my older brother's friends to Kentucky Lake and they would catch so many crappie that they filled ten-gallon milk cans with fish.

Then Dad bought a trailer and put it at Reelfoot Lake where we came to know a gentleman named Elbert Spicer. Mr. Elbert was a legend. He'd called and hunted ducks with the very best of the very best. For decades. Until, when he was in his seventies, he decided he was going to die. Then he went to bed to die. After several months passed, he decided maybe he was not going to die, at least not yet. So he got out of the bed and took up where he had left off: drinking whiskey, chasing young women too young to be his granddaughters, hunting ducks, and fishing.

Mr. Elbert knew where the fish were and how to catch them. One day he said to Mother, "Mrs. Judge, the crappie are gettin' 'bout right. If you'd like to go, I'd be proud to take you."

Mother instantly knew two things. First, he was not trying to get her alone, since she was but thirty years his junior and far too old to interest him. Second, he could catch fish. So they took off for one of Mr. Elbert's favorite spots. He took Mom's cane pole, placed the minnows on double hooks, and before he could get his own pole baited, Mom was catching fish.

When Mom would swing the pole up and the line and fish over the boat, Mr. Elbert would grab the crappie and take it off the hook, rebait Mom's hook, and put her in business again. He'd paddle the boat back where he wanted it, but before he could get his own line in the water, Mom would have another fish—or two—and his work would start over again. Finally Mr. Elbert could stand it no longer:

"Mrs. Judge," he begged, "do you reckon you'd mind if I fished a little, too?"

"Well, of course not, Mr. Spicer," Mom replied. "I've been baiting my own hooks and taking my own fish off for forty years and I don't mind a bit."

Soon they both were pulling in fish as fast as they could, and competing to see who could catch the most. They argued for years over who won.

* * *

Mother has always loved to go. It didn't matter where, she was ready. That was good, because Dad often would come home and say, "Let's go," and we would.

When my younger brother Ben and I were in high school, our parents went to Europe. While they were gone, Ben started riding Brahma bulls and bareback broncs—he is, after all, Mother's son. When they learned of Ben's new hobby, Dad was delighted, his own father having been a cowboy out West for a time. Mother, however, was not amused. In fact, she was terrified that her baby was climbing on huge Brahma bulls. Some years went by before she would take another long trip. Finally, when we were both in college, our parents went away for ten days. Ben immediately planned to start sky-diving. Unfortunately, his scheduled jumps were rained out, and even Ben would not try it with Mom and Dad back home. Ben really is Mother's son and the far bravest child. His idea of fun now is kayaking the roughest water in the Eastern U.S. or going for still wilder streams in Colorado.

* * *

In 1976, Dad and Mom bought a new pickup and went to Alaska. By the next spring, he was gone. We children all thought that when Dad died, Mother might not be far behind. Instead, she began the mourning that continues to this day, and then she went on living.

She began by going to Hawaii. She also took her first cruise. In her late sixties, she started riding buses to visit her children and grandchildren. In her seventies, she first rafted white water. And she started fishing again. In her seventy-eighth year, my brother Dean took her fishing at his home on Timms Ford Lake. At his boat dock, he fixed Mom up with a cane pole, but she could not see the bobber. For over twenty years Mother has been losing her sight to macular degeneration. She has some peripheral vision, but essentially now can see only light and dark. So, she got down on her hands and knees on the dock, put her face so close to the water her head almost touched the bobber, and held the fishing line in her hands.

Soon she had a bite and with a joyous squeal she yanked the line and pulled out a big bream. Immediately after Dean pulled the fish off her hook and helped her rebait, she was back on her hands and knees, face close to the bobber. In a few minutes she caught a half dozen bream, as happy as if she'd caught Moby Dick.

* * *

Even as she has gone blind, she has continued to live at home and alone, fiercely independent, strong even in weakness and perhaps especially in adversity, tough as any. A few days after the family gathered for Mother's eightieth birthday party, she went to the doctor. Not eagerly, not even willingly, but only after my wife Nancy learned Mother had fallen in the yard and had to be helped back in the house. When the reluctant patient heard the cardiologist say that a pacemaker might restore her energy and strength, she wanted the surgery that day, only grudgingly consenting to wait five days. Dr. Hall explained that the pacemaker's battery would last eight years and then would have to be replaced. My mother's only question was, "Can you do that replacement here also?"

* * *

Not long ago, Mother needed to go back into the hospital. She dreaded the visit, but knew something was wrong. She got her courage up once again, telling Nancy and me, "I want to stick around long enough for your boys to remember me. They're my reason for living."

Loving children has long been her reason for living.

* * *

I marvel that a woman who lives in the same house where she grew up, and frequently sleeps on the same bed where she gave birth to her firstborn, is always so eager to go. In recent years, sometimes her eagerness has been dampened a bit by her sense of propriety. It embarasses her to go out to eat because she cannot see the food and is terrified she might spill something. Still, she frequently screws up her courage, puts on her panty-hose, and takes off on a new adventure.

Recently, Mother flew in a small plane, the first time since her father and the barnstormer took her aloft seventy years earlier. Last year, the year she turned eighty-two, I asked what she wanted for a Mother's Day gift. We gathered her four children and her youngest grandchildren. Then, for the first time in the more than two decades since Dad died, she fished at Reelfoot Lake.

Knowing how much she enjoyed that fishing trip and thinking we might again do something similar, the other day I asked Mother what fun things she'd like to do that she had not yet done.

She told me she would like to go up in a hot–air balloon, pilot a plane, and go to the moon.

TEN

A Double Portion
of Thy Spirit

*A*fter sixty-four years close to the land and forty-three years of marriage, my father seldom varied his daily routine. I knew his customs well from twenty-three years as his son. Mother, of course, knew his habits even better than I did and she also was home with him that last morning. We know what happened, even before Mother awakened and after Dad left, the same way you know what your own heart is saying.

* * *

On his last morning, as always, Dad awoke long before dawn.

He put his hand gently on his four-year-old grandson's back and rubbed softly, just like he had rubbed my back so many times. His only daughter and her husband had named the child Will. Everyone in the family agreed that Will looked just like Dad's third son, my brother Ben, which meant Will also looked just like the photos taken of Dad when he was a child. On the other side of the boy, Mother was asleep.

About the time the clock glowed four o'clock, Dad turned on the light. He put a pillow beside the grand-boy's face to shadow him. Mother raised up, looked at the clock, murmured "Good morning," and pulled a pillow over her head.

Dad went to the kitchen and got coffee in his large, thick cup, which he had proudly told me was made from clay mined in our home county by a company that had been his client before he became a judge. As usual, he lay back in bed to sip his black coffee and read. First, the hunter and fisherman enjoyed *Field and Stream* and *Outdoor Life*. Then the trial court judge studied the most recent decisions of Tennessee's courts of appeal and supreme court in the periodical *Southwestern Reporter*.

As the sunlight began to filter through the curtains, the farmer rose and put on his baggy khaki work pants and an old blue and white short-sleeved dress shirt that even he realized was not fit for wearing to court any more, not even under a black robe. He sat on the bed and pulled on his black, specially made, orthopedic shoes with the rubber soles and curved insteps. Then, to her surprise, he told Mother she ought not go with him to feed the cattle, though they always did that together on glorious spring Sunday mornings like this one.

Dad said Mother should stay home with "our boy," since Will had a cold. She thought it odd, since they had planned to go together. The night before, Dad had even asked Will if he wanted to go, and Will had replied, as Dad had taught him, "Sho, sho," which was grandfather-talk for "Sure, sure." But now Dad said, No, no, he would go alone and she should stay there and take care of the grandboy. He would be back soon, in plenty of time for Sunday School.

* * *

It had been but a couple of years since Dad's Uncle Dean had passed. Uncle Dean had lived not far from us and not far from our farm, outside of Greenfield in a big, brick house his grandfather built right after the Civil War. The house seemed so grand some said it looked not quite at home on the gently sloping Tennessee farmland, but rather ought to have been on top of a big hill, demanding respect. Still, Uncle Dean always seemed to fit that stately house.

Uncle Dean was such a gentleman that even when his sister, Dad's mother, pulled a pistol on him, he just quietly told her, "Grace, put that thing away." He earned the respect of his neighbors so completely that they elected him a justice of the peace for four decades and put him on the county court for three. Part of that time he also was a state representative and a state senator. He gained the respect and earned the friendship of Governor Gordon Browning and Congressman Ed Jones and many others who knew his character and integrity.

Dad loved Uncle Dean so much that he named his firstborn, my older brother, for him. Decades later Dad watched this same Uncle Dean die slowly, his circulation failing so that doctors had to cut off part of one leg. And

then another part. And then the other leg, so he was left
with stumps. Uncle Dean went piece by piece, and Dad
saw it happen. And he had seen many others linger long
and suffer much. Dad knew well that there were better
and worse ways to die.

* * *

For years my father had hammered his heart daily
with three packs of Camels. A heart attack when he was
fifty-four brought him, the doctor said, within ten minutes of death. As he lay in a hospital bed, the doctor told
him if he wanted to see my younger brother Ben and me
grow up, he had best not smoke another coffin nail. And
he quit. Right then.

That gave him almost another decade. Almost, but
not quite.

His heart also had been loaded down with decades of
fine Southern cooking, the kind of fat-rich foods eaten by
poor folks and by many who lived through, but never
past, tough times. Dad didn't believe in wasting any of
the hog, not after living through the Depression when
farmers couldn't afford to eat their own livestock. When
times got better, he ate all the pork and beef he could
afford. And he knew the times were good when he could
afford to drink the thick, tasty cream, and the thick, stout
buttermilk. He loved the kind of cooking that some can
survive no matter, but many of us can handle only if we
labor hard and burn the fat before it clogs our arteries.
Dad had been a part-time farmer and a full-time office
sitter too long.

His thirty-three years of pain had taken their toll on
his heart as well. From the minute he regained con-

sciousness after the mortar shell landed in Belgium in 1944 until this spring morning in 1977, every waking moment was filled with pain.

Finally, there were his genes, the same genes that had brought heart disease and untimely deaths to too many in his family.

This history made for congestive heart failure that was causing fluid to build within him. He was slowly drowning in fluids that his heart could not pump off.

He did not want to lie, like Uncle Dean had, in some nursing home. And he did not want to lie doped up and connected to countless tubes in a hospital with his life not really extended but only his death protracted; he had been in more than enough hospitals since the war.

And he knew he was dying. He had told Mother he did not think he would be around much longer, trying to prepare her. He had also tried, unsuccessfully, to hurry me through college and straight into law school. But he had never said why he was in a hurry for me to finish, and I'd been too thick to understand, too confident that my father, who had survived so much would, of course, be around for a long time. He had gone over details pertaining to the farms with my brother Ben and me. He had tried to get his business matters in order. He had written and re-written his will.

On this morning, he knew, somehow, that his time had come. And so, he embraced the time. To do so that Sunday morning, he had to carefully and caringly push away those he loved.

He hugged and kissed his precious youngest grandson for the last time, as Will slept.

His Mary Cornelia looked into the bluest eyes she had

ever seen, surrounded by the longest eyelashes she had ever seen on a man. He held and kissed her. He reassured her. No, he would go to the farm alone, not to worry, just take good care of that Grandboy—isn't he precious, aren't we blessed? He would just feed the cattle some corn, count 'em to make sure they were okay, and see if there were any new calves. He would be back soon, he said. I guess he knew he would be, one way or another.

Dad drove the tan and white Chevrolet pickup truck. He had bought it the year before to go to Alaska with Mother, a trip they had long dreamed about. Dad had wanted me to go with them, but I had just returned from a year in Europe and wanted to be home before law school started in a few days.

* * *

That morning, Dad drove the pickup to the Kimery Road farm, near the forks of the river, a mile or so from the farmhouse where he had started out not quite sixty-five years earlier.

He turned at Kimery Store, the old country store his parents had owned. Biblical prophecies had almost come to fulfillment at the store, which also had served as a polling place on election days. There if the dead did not exactly get up and walk, they sure seemed to vote a lot.

He drove past the brush pile and the woods lot where he'd taken me to find the covey of quail that was almost always nearby. That was the covey that provided my first quail when Dad first took me, a ten-year-old carrying my grandfather's 20-gauge Remington pump shotgun.

He parked the truck on the side of the road where he always did. He climbed the fence, then walked past the buttercups, more buttercups than one could count and so yellow that they painted the end of the field where the old house had stood. As he walked on the soft ground to the grain bin, he looked past the barn to the pear orchard that had been created before he was. Above the gnarled old pear trees was a bright blue sky. He called out, and the brown and white Hereford cattle ambled across the green pasture toward him.

The earth was warming and coming alive again. The early sunlight fell gently on him as he took the bucket of yellow corn from the grain bin for the cattle. I hope he fell gently as he returned to that earth again. A heart attack took him.

I believe my father went to the farm to die that morning. He did what he did not want to do. But he did what he had to do. And he did it when and where and how he wanted. He fell on his favorite farm, at his favorite time of year, on a glorious and beautiful day, in the quiet and peace of early morning, on the sacred Sabbath. And no one, most especially Mother, had to watch him die.

Ashes to ashes, dust to dust, Scripture says. Son of the soil back to the soil. The farmer to the farm.

* * *

I was in my first year of law school, living in Nashville. When I was home for Christmas, Mother had quietly said she thought Dad would not live much longer. I don't know why, but I just would not believe her. About that same time, someone at the law school kindly thought of me when a woman wanted a law student to come live for free with her recently widowed father, a lawyer. My new landlord and housemate, Mr. Casey, was eighty-four years old. When the phone rang that March morning as we were getting ready for church, I thought maybe it was one of the widows that had been calling him.

Indeed, it was a widow—my mother. She told me the news. "Your father has had another heart attack. They found him down at the farm. He's gone. He didn't suffer any, they say."

I told Mother I'd be right home, told her I loved her, reassured her that, yes, ma'am, certainly I'd drive safely. Then I told Mr. Casey the news. I got my suit and a tie and toilet bag and got in the car. I drove west the two and a half hours. When I could, I sang "Amazing Grace." Over and over. But most of the time I couldn't. I missed Dad too much.

At home, the driveway already was full, so I parked in front of the house and walked up the steps Dad had struggled up when he came home from the war. On the front porch was Ricky, my friend since kindergarten, who already had lost his father. As I hugged Ricky, over his shoulder I saw Wayne Fisher, who served as Dad's clerk and master. Tears were in Mr. Fisher's eyes as I embraced him. Then I went to the back bedroom and found Mother.

* * *

On March 15, we went about burying my Dad. For my father's funeral, the Dresden First United Methodist Church sanctuary was full and then some. Several who did not come early, and all those who came late, stood outside. Just as Dad had requested, our neighbor, Miss Toni, sang "The Old Rugged Cross."

We sat on the front center pew—my older and younger brothers, my sister, my mother, and I. Right behind us sat my brother Dean's wife, Dad's three grandsons, his sister, and other family. Dad's casket, covered with an American flag, was a few feet in front of us.

The pastor, Brother Anderson, was a kindly, older cherub with the gentlest of spirits. Some would have said preaching was not his strongest gift. That day they would have been wrong. He talked of Dad's passion for justice and his compassion for the weak, his sense of equity and fairness, his concern for the less fortunate and the hurting. Then the preacher reminded us that his good deeds and kind ways did not have to die with him.

Brother Anderson preached from the second chapter of Second Kings, telling the story of the prophets Elijah and Elisha. The older Elijah knew that he was at the end of his time on earth and repeatedly tried to get Elisha to leave him. But each time, Elisha replied, "As the Lord lives, and as you yourself live, I will not leave you." Finally, after they crossed the Jordan River and just before Elijah was taken up into heaven, he said to Elisha, "Ask what I shall do for you, before I am taken from you."

To which Elisha replied, "I pray you, let me inherit a double share of your spirit."

It was up to us, Brother Anderson said, and to all who had been touched by my father, to ask for a double share of his spirit. And it was up to us to carry on his work and his life. The preacher said that Dad did not have to die, not even on earth. Not as long as we took his life and love, and ourselves lived and loved.

Theologians and preachers say a great deal about eternal life. They tell many things about heaven, streets of gold, mansions on high. I had read and heard those things all my life. But this much I realized sitting in front of that flag-draped coffin: As long as Dad's children and grandchildren and their children live, My father could live. As long as we love, Dad's life and love will not die.